Backcountry Skiing Adventures

CLASSIC SKI AND SNOWBOARD TOURS
IN VERMONT AND NEW YORK

ALSO AVAILABLE FROM
APPALACHIAN MOUNTAIN CLUB BOOKS

Backcountry Skiing Adventures: Classic Ski and Snowboard Tours in
Maine and New Hampshire
by David Goodman

Winter Camping, 2d edition
by Stephen Gorman

Ultimate Guide to Backcountry Travel
by Michael Lanza

Into the Mountains
by Maggie Stier and Ron McAdow

North Woods
by Peter J. Marchand

Backcountry Skiing Adventures

CLASSIC SKI AND SNOWBOARD TOURS IN VERMONT AND NEW YORK

David Goodman

APPALACHIAN MOUNTAIN CLUB BOOKS
BOSTON, MASSACHUSETTS

Cover Photographs: Chuck Waskuch
Front cover photo: Telemark skiing on the summit of Mt. Mansfield, Vermont.
All inside photographs by the author unless otherwise noted
Cover Design: Elisabeth Leydon Brady
Book Design: Carol Bast Tyler

Excerpts from Alice E. Johannsen, *The Legendary Jackrabbit Johannsen*
(Montreal: McGill-Queen's University Press, 1993)
reprinted with permission of the publisher.

Distributed by The Globe Pequot Press, Inc., Guilford, CT

Library of Congress Cataloging-in-Publication Data
Goodman, David, 1959-
Backcountry skiing adventures : classic ski and snowboard tours in Vermont and New York /
David Goodman ; [all photographs by author unless otherwise noted].
p. cm.
Includes bibliographical references.
ISBN 1-878239-70-8 (alk. paper)
1. Cross-country skiing--Vermont--Guidebooks. 2. Cross-country skiing--New York--Guidebooks.
3. Snowboarding--Vermont--Guidebooks. 4. Snowboarding--New York--Guidebooks. 5. Vermont--
Guidebooks. 6. New York--Guidebooks. I. Title.
GV854.5.V5 G66 2000
796.93'2'09743--dc21   00-064005

The paper used in this publication meets the minimum requirements of the
American National Standard for Information Sciences—Permanence of Paper for
Printed Library Materials, ANSI Z39.48–1984.∞

**Due to changes in conditions,
use of the information in this book
is at the sole risk of the user.**

Printed on recycled paper using soy-based inks.
Printed in the United States of America.

10 9 8 7 6 5 4 3 2 1   98 99 00 01 02 03

Contents

To Bill,
who loves a great adventure

Preface

This book is the product of several passions. When I was a college student in the early 1980s, I went on my first cross-country ski outings with friends. We would go to Lincoln Woods around Boston or up to the White Mountains in New Hampshire and glide around the forest. I marveled at how my friends, who had been skiing for years, could move so gracefully on snow. I learned by mimicking them and became proficient through trial and error. My flirtation with skiing quickly became an infatuation.

The high mountains have been another passion. My hikes in the mountains of the Northeast led to rock and ice climbing and mountaineering throughout North America and beyond. I have been intoxicated by the high and wild places of the planet. The freedom, the challenge, the special camaraderie shared with friends in the mountains, and the sheer joy of being in a remote setting have been a constant lure. I managed to combine work and pleasure for a number of years working as a mountaineering instructor for the Hurricane Island Outward Bound School. This kept me in the wild place I love most—my home mountains of New England.

Inevitably skis and high mountains converged. Backcountry skiing has been a way for me to bring together my quest for big mountains and my addiction to the sensual thrill of skiing. In the great tradition of backcountry skiing, I learned my most enduring lessons with my head buried deeply in the eastern snowpack. Slowly and stubbornly, I figured out how to ski the fickle snows of the Northeast.

The Appalachian Mountain Club approached me in 1987 and asked if I would write a book about skiing in New England. The editors, perhaps foolishly, left it to my discretion how to approach the subject. I decided to write a historical guidebook about skiing in the highest mountains of New England. These were the places that everyone except snowshoers and a few die-hard telemarkers assumed were inaccessible in winter. But I knew that skiers had been crisscrossing the high peaks of the Northeast since the 1920s. The problem was that it had been a half-century since the heyday of such "down-mountain skiing." I had a great deal of fun doing the ski research that winter. And I figured the book would have a loyal audience of about 200 fellow telemark fanatics.

Classic Backcountry Skiing: A Guide to the Best Ski Tours in New England was published by the AMC in December 1988. After it appeared, something happened that I didn't anticipate: a lot of people read the book. At trailheads around New England, I have come across snow-covered cars with tattered copies of the guidebook lying on the dashboard. The book even garnered two national ski-writing awards.

Classic Backcountry Skiing arrived just as telemark skiing was starting to boom. People were looking for alternatives to the increasingly homogenized downhill ski scene. They found it right in their own backyards, often on ski trails that had been around for a half-century or more.

A dozen years later, it is time for a fresh look at backcountry skiing in the Northeast. Many things have changed since the original book. Trails have been rerouted, renamed, opened, and closed. Some tours that I wrote about in the first book did not, on subsequent visits, inspire me enough to include them again. Backcountry skiing is now a popular pastime, and telemarkers have become remarkably proficient and creative skiers. People are searching farther afield for ski terrain, and that is a good sign. This guide is intended merely to open the door to the world of backcountry *glisse*, or sliding. The joy of exploration is left to you.

One of the more significant developments since publication of the last book is the explosion in popularity of snowboarding. Increasingly, skiers and snowboarders are sharing the trail in their pursuit of the deepest snow and highest summits. Snowboarders are now in the position that skiers were in during the 1980s: They are seeking freedom, looking for wilder snow. This guide helps point the way.

Backcountry Skiing Adventures builds on the groundwork laid by *Classic Backcountry Skiing*. Many of the present tour descriptions draw heavily upon information that originally appeared in the earlier edition. But there are many new tours and a considerable amount of updated information about old tours. Every tour description has changed, often significantly.

The sheer quantity of great ski terrain in the Northeast has burgeoned to the point where one guidebook is no longer adequate. *Backcountry Skiing Adventures* has been published in two volumes. *Backcountry Skiing Adventures: Classic Ski and Snowboard Tours in Maine and New Hampshire* covers the great skiing and snowboarding in the northeastern half of New England. This guidebook covers backcountry skiing and snowboarding in Vermont, a classic tour in western Massachusetts, and finally ventures across Lake Champlain to probe the secrets of one of the East's greatest mountain ranges, the Adirondacks.

May your mountain journeys be deep.

Acknowledgments

I am grateful to a number of people for their help with the research for this book. Their assistance ranged from joining me on the many miles of trail that I covered to fact-checking certain tours. Thanks to my ski partners, including Barry Goodman, Kim Brown, Eric Scranton, Kate Carter, Jeff Parsons, Chris Hyson, and Steve and Nan Amstutz. To all of you, I offer my gratitude for coming along and apologies for poaching first tracks.

I am indebted to several people who reviewed parts of this book and offered valuable comments: Ben Rose at the Green Mountain Club, Chris Mask at Burton Snowboards, Rich Thompson Tucker at Merck Forest, and Blair Mahar of Big Schuss Productions. Special thanks to Jeff Leich of the New England Ski Museum for his help over the years with my ski research, and to Tony Goodwin of the Adirondack Ski Touring Council, who provided invaluable help both on and off the trail with my Adirondack research. Beth Krusi and Elisabeth Brady—the editor and production manager, respectively, at AMC Books—have been insightful and enthusiastic shepherds of this book.

I owe special thanks to Todd Eastman. It was while working together as instructors for Outward Bound in the Adirondacks in the 1980s that he first told me tales of the adventures of the Adirondack Ski to Die Club. He encouraged me to write about the renaissance of backcountry skiing in the Northeast. I have been doing it ever since.

I have kept a vow of silence about the great skiing in the Adirondacks for twenty years. I figured that was long enough. To Ski-to-Diers Anne and Dave Hough and Robbie Frenette, thanks for blazing the way and sharing your maniacal passion for these hills. I hope you don't mind me revealing a few Adirondack pearls here, but if you do, please don't break my skis.

My deepest thanks go to my family. Sue Minter, my wife, fellow explorer, and skiing inspiration, has made this book possible by all the support she has given and the passion for the mountains we have shared. My son, Jasper, who arrived during the winter that I wrote this, and my daughter, Ariel, hopefully will find the same pleasure in these mountains in the coming years that I have.

This book is dedicated to Bill Minter, my partner, beau frère, and friend on more adventures over the years than I can count. We've shared the thrill at being lost and found in many a high and wild place. No road trip has been too long for him, no trail talk too boring, and no jump too high for him to leap. Here's to all the first tracks I stole that were rightfully his—and to many more journeys ahead.

Author's Note

This book is about adventures in snow. It is intended for use by both skiers (including freeheel and randonée) and snowboarders. The spirit of this book is captured by the French word *glisse*, which is derived from *glisser*—literally, "to slide." Sliding on snow is the essence of our sport. This book is a history, guide, and celebration of Northeastern *glisse* in all its forms.

My tour descriptions rely largely on the language of skiing. That is inevitable: skiing is the oldest of the *glisse* disciplines and skiers constitute the majority of backcountry *glisse* practitioners. The Northeast is also steeped in a rich ski history, which I chronicle throughout these chapters.

In the interest of simplicity and consistency, I use "skiing" throughout this book to refer to traveling on snow, whether it be on skis or snowboards. The exceptions to this practice should be apparent, such as when I address issues of specific concern to skiers or snowboarders, particularly in the area of technique and equipment.

Map of Tour Locations

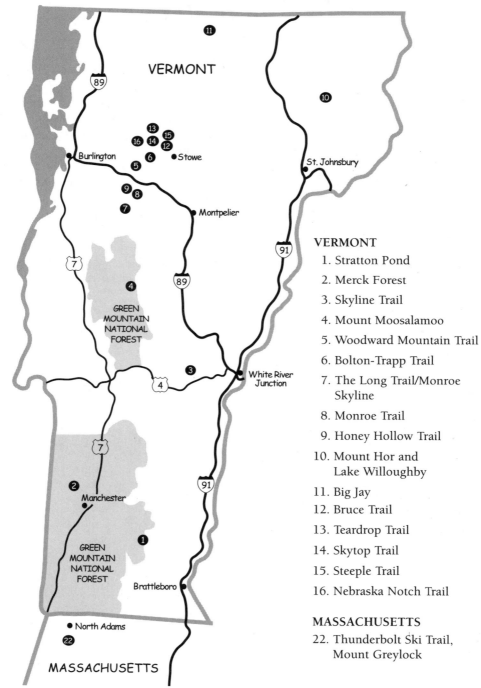

VERMONT

1. Stratton Pond
2. Merck Forest
3. Skyline Trail
4. Mount Moosalamoo
5. Woodward Mountain Trail
6. Bolton-Trapp Trail
7. The Long Trail/Monroe Skyline
8. Monroe Trail
9. Honey Hollow Trail
10. Mount Hor and Lake Willoughby
11. Big Jay
12. Bruce Trail
13. Teardrop Trail
14. Skytop Trail
15. Steeple Trail
16. Nebraska Notch Trail

MASSACHUSETTS

22. Thunderbolt Ski Trail, Mount Greylock

NEW YORK

17. Jackrabbit Trail

18. Camp Peggy O'Brien Hut Tour

19. Wright Peak Ski Trail

20. Avalanche Pass

21. Mount Marcy

SECTION ONE

The Backcountry World

The Backcountry World

WELCOME TO THE WORLD OF BACKCOUNTRY GLISSE.

Glisse—derived from the French word that means "to slide"—encompasses all the ways that we enjoy and explore snow. The backcountry today is shared by sliders of every variety, from skiers to snowboarders. Who knows what new inventions will come along in future years that will further expand our enjoyment of the snowy world? I embrace them all in this book. The ethic of all these disciplines is that you earn your turns: When you climb a mountain under your own steam, you have earned the right to descend in whatever manner you find most aesthetic and pleasurable, provided it does not harm the mountain environment.

Skiers and snowboarders have a shared passion: the love of the backcountry world in winter. This world is familiar to many of you. It is the hiking trails you climb in summer. The mountain summits you stop to admire. The trails you wonder about when you look on a map. It includes trailless peaks and well-trodden mountain paths.

To others, this is a new place. You may have been skiing at ski touring centers at the base of the big peaks. Or you have been snowboarding on the "front side" of many of these mountains, possibly curious about the other side of the hill—the one without chairlifts. This book is about that world.

Backcountry *glisse* is the full spectrum of traveling on snow: going uphill, downhill, across mountain summits, along river valleys. It is skiing and snowboarding off of groomed trails and prepared snow. This style of travel goes by many names. Some call it ski or snowboard mountaineering; others call it off-piste (off-trail) skiing or snowboarding, ski touring, mountain skiing, randonée, alpine touring, telemarking, Nordic skiing, or cross-country skiing. In some ways, this mode of travel encompasses all of the above; in other ways, it resists easy categorization. Seventy years ago it was all simply called skiing. In spirit—*glisse*—it is all one sport.

Skiers today will find that Nordic ski equipment—so-called telemark gear— is unmatched in providing an efficient and enjoyable means of travel to reach the best untouched snow in remote places. But the ski techniques, which include telemark and parallel turns, are a hybrid of cross-country and downhill. Backcountry skiing is done in the high mountains, which naturally means that skiing downhill is a major part of the experience and the thrill. "Down-mountain skiing" was the term that skiers from the 1930s used to describe this style of downhill skiing in the backcountry.

3

Snowboarders heading into the backcountry are pioneering new ground. Snowboarders follow in tracks blazed by skiers in earlier years, but they travel with new tools and a fresh eye for adventure. They may come in search of a streambed shaped like a natural half-pipe. They may seek out remote, powdery, steep descents. Or perhaps they are content to tour up, down, and wherever the mountain leads them. Riders and skiers are united in their quest for solitude, untracked snow, and a wilder experience.

Backcountry *glisse* is full of surprises. You can glide to quiet places where the snow is untracked, perhaps changing texture with each mile. Your skis, snowshoes, or snowboards also can take you to exciting places, such as high summits with breathtaking snowfields and expansive views.

Backcountry travelers embark on a journey, but there is not necessarily a destination. Be open to whatever comes along. Sometimes the goal of the journey is introspection and solitude. Other times, the goal is simply to enjoy traveling under your own power through the winter wilderness. Often we go just to have fun. Whatever your motivations, the backcountry journey requires an exploratory mindset. Bring a spirit of adventure and accept that not everything will turn out quite as planned. Just as the character of a trail changes with each storm, the experience you have each time you fasten on skis or a snowboard and head into the mountains is never the same as it was before.

The tradition of backcountry skiing and snowboarding in the mountains of the Northeast dates back nearly a century. By the 1930s, the search for the perfect ski run down a mountain was underway in every corner of the Northeast. The highest peaks of the North Country—Mount Marcy, Mount Mansfield, Mount Washington, Mount Cardigan, Mount Greylock—all became home to famous ski trails. These trails, with names like Thunderbolt, Nose Dive, Teardrop, and Wildcat, still bring a surge of adrenaline and satisfaction to riders and skiers today. But since the mid-1940s, skiing has become fragmented into narrow niches: cross-country skiers have stayed on the fields and old logging roads, while downhill skiers and snowboarders have been riding chairlifts to get to their ski trails. Most skiers have considered wilderness areas and the high mountains to be inaccessible.

My intent with this book is to encourage skiers and snowboarders to return once again to the high and wild places of the Northeast. I try to recapture the spirit of adventure that led the skiers of an earlier generation to head to the mountains and explore. The tours in this book are only a sampling.

Numerous other peaks, open woods, slides, and drainages offer first-rate skiing and snowboarding to those willing to adventure. Indeed, your own backyard may hold unexplored riches. The world of backcountry *glisse* is, after all, every place where it is white.

The Northeastern Renaissance

Every time skiers or snowboarders push off from a trailhead and vanish into a winter wilderness, we feel like explorers setting off for the New World, as if we were the first visitors to these wild places. But if the snow could speak, it would tell a different story. It would simply welcome us back. For we are merely traveling in the tracks of skiers who plied these routes for decades and then mysteriously vanished.

Backcountry skiing is not a new sport in the Northeast. It is actually a revival of a sport that enjoyed its heyday in the 1930s and has been in a period of dormancy until recently.

The first skiers in New England were Scandinavian loggers and railroad builders in the mid-1800s. They formed the first ski club in the United States in Berlin, New Hampshire, in 1882. It was later named the Fridtjof Nansen Ski Club, after the famous Norwegian Arctic explorer who skied across Greenland in 1888. Skis began appearing in Hanover, New Hampshire, and in North Adams, Massachusetts, by the turn of the century, and the popularity of the sport slowly began to pick up.

Mountain skiing began attracting interest soon after people gained some basic proficiency with the unwieldy new mode of transportation. The first ski ascent and descent of Mount Marcy in the Adirondacks was accomplished in 1911. Mount Washington was skied (via today's auto road) in 1913. And Mount Mansfield in Vermont was first skied in 1914 via the Toll Road. Ski racing began gaining interest at Dartmouth College in Hanover, New Hampshire, around the same time.

Skiers of this early era would immerse themselves in all aspects of the sport. They were typically proficient at ski jumping, downhill, slalom, and cross-country skiing, sometimes called *langlauf* ("long-run") skiing. Since people would use the same skis for everything, there was little difference between cross-country and downhill skiing except where people chose to ski. In the 1920s, ski bindings consisted of a toe bar with a leather heel strap, much like today's cable bindings. Skis were long, heavy hickory boards without metal edges, and boots were the leather hiking-style variety with a box-shaped toe.

Throughout the 1920s, eastern skiers looking for downhill skiing opportunities sought out narrow summer hiking trails, logging roads, and streambeds. This was not easy terrain to ski, and skiers soon began searching for more open downhill slopes. Katharine Peckett, daughter of the affluent owner of an inn near Franconia, New Hampshire, decided after returning from a vacation in Switzerland to clear a small hill near her father's inn. She opened the first ski school in the United States in 1929. It was around this same time that skiers began to make forays into Tuckerman Ravine. The first official downhill race in the country was held on Mount Moosilauke in New Hampshire in 1927. While ski touring through the woods was still an enjoyable pastime, skiers were increasingly drawn to the thrill of a good downhill run, and they would travel long and far to find the mountains with the best downhill skiing.

By the 1930s, skiing had captured the imagination of New Englanders. In 1931, the first "snow trains" for skiers left North Station in Boston headed for New Hampshire, and snow trains to Vermont began rolling out of New York City. Within its first year of operation, the Boston & Maine snow train transported 8,371 passengers to New Hampshire. More than 10,000 skiers boarded the train the following year, and by 1935 the snow trains were taking 22,240 people north.

Equipment evolved to keep pace with the rising interest in downhill skiing. Skis with metal edges appeared, and steel cable bindings were introduced. These bindings offered the option of latching down the heel cable for descending on steeper terrain.

A major catalyst for ski activity in the region came about as a direct result of the Depression. The Civilian Conservation Corps (CCC) was created by President Franklin Roosevelt in March 1933 to provide work for unemployed men. It had the dual purpose of addressing national conservation needs and providing jobs. Recruits were drawn primarily from families on the relief rolls, and each man earned $30 per month for his work, of which about $25 went to his dependents.

The CCC was in existence from 1933 to 1942. Some 2.5 million men passed through "Roosevelt's Forest Army," making it the largest peacetime government labor force in American history. The "CCC boys" improved millions of acres of forest and parkland, built roads, constructed irrigation systems throughout the West, fought forest fires, and provided disaster assistance. Their most visible and enduring legacy is the parks they built. In the South, thirteen states had no state parks and half had no parks at all in 1933; within six years, the CCC had built parks in ten of those states. The CCC ultimately developed hundreds of national, state, county, and municipal parks around the country.

The CCC will be remembered best by New England skiers for the numerous ski trails that it built. Vermont was the greatest beneficiary in this regard, since the state's CCC contingent was under the supervision of Perry Merrill, an avid skier. Under Merrill's direction the CCC cut some of the most famous ski runs in the East. Among the trails that still endure are the Nose Dive, Teardrop, Bruce, Ski Meister, Perry Merrill, and (Charlie) Lord trails on Mount Mansfield. In New Hampshire, the CCC's contributions include the Richard Taft Trail on Cannon Mountain, the Alexandria Trail on Mount Cardigan, the Gulf of Slides Trail near Mount Washington, and the Wildcat Trail on the north side of Wildcat Mountain. Many of the CCC's contributions to skiing in New England are cited elsewhere in this book.

Charlie Lord was the master designer of the CCC trails on Mount Mansfield. Lord, who died in 1997 at the age of ninety-five, once explained to me his formula for creating the high-quality runs for which the CCC became famous: "The only guide we had was we tried to make them interesting for ourselves. We were a selfish bunch, you know. The trails were made for a fairly good skier—not experts, but we tried to pick a route that would challenge us." Very few of the CCC men were actually skiers, since skiing was even then a sport of the middle and upper classes. "But," said Lord, "some of them were quite enthused about skiing" and enjoyed coming out to watch the big ski races that took place on their trails.

The construction of the CCC ski trails initiated a new era of "down-mountain skiing." This was the term used to describe downhill skiing in the backcountry. Down-mountain trails, also called "walk-up" trails because skiers had to hike up in order to ski down them, defined the character of skiing in the early 1930s. On some of the longer trails, such as the Bruce Trail on Mount Mansfield, hiking up and skiing down just once took a full day. These outings were often equal parts mountaineering and skiing adventures.

A few select trails were challenging enough to merit classification as Class A race trails. Class A trails had to be 1.0 to 1.5 miles long, with a vertical drop of 2,000 feet and at least one section with a gradient of 30 to 35 degrees. The Class A trails of the Northeast included the Nose Dive, Richard Taft Trail, Wildcat Trail, Whiteface Trail on Whiteface Mountain, Thunderbolt Trail on Mount Greylock, and the Pine Hill Trail on Wachusett Mountain. These were the only trails where a racer could receive a coveted rating based on his or her time. "A" racers were the fastest, while "B" and "C" racers were close behind.

Ski technique was evolving from telemark and snowplow to styles more suited to racing. Christiania and stem turns, which marked the beginnings of parallel ski technique, were being advocated by the better coaches. Skiers quickly abandoned the graceful old telemark in favor of the faster parallel turn.

The popularity of the CCC trails also signaled a subtle change in the direction that skiing was taking. Exploration of the mountains on skis was taking a backseat to skiing on the established down-mountain trails. These wide ski trails were simply a joy to ski. They were a welcome alternative to negotiating difficult hiking trails.

Abner Coleman confessed in the Appalachian Mountain Club journal, *Appalachia,* in 1936:

> The direction of the movement in Vermont is following the widespread preference for downhill running. To some extent this delightful obsession is unfortunate, if only because it leaves a lot of ideal terrain to the mercy of snowshoers.

The winter countryside is but little used even by those who live in it. The stampede, rather, both of natives and visitors, has been toward the localities providing down-mountain runs.

The heyday of the down-mountain trails was relatively brief. In 1934, the first rope tow was introduced at a ski hill in Woodstock, Vermont. Within seven years, J-bars, T-bars, and chairlifts sprang up on almost every major ski mountain in New England. In 1938 an aerial tramway was erected on Cannon Mountain in New Hampshire, and two years later Mount Mansfield in Stowe became home to the longest chairlift in the country. The CCC trails often became the nucleus of the new downhill ski areas, as was the case with the Nose Dive on Mount Mansfield, the Wildcat Trail in the Wildcat Ski Area, and the Richard Taft Trail in the Cannon Mountain Ski Area. Those trails that were not crowned with a chairlift were often abandoned, to be reclaimed by weeds and shrubs. This was the fate of a number of trails, including the original Chin Clip on Mount Mansfield and the now defunct Katzensteig Trail on Wildcat Mountain.

But many of the down-mountain trails survived. Some, like the Snapper Trail on Mount Moosilauke, were preserved as hiking trails, while others, such as the Teardrop and Bruce trails on Mount Mansfield and the Tucker Brook Trail on Cannon Mountain, were maintained by dedicated local skiers. These people often cleared the trails in defiance of new state and federal regulations that forbade skiing on trails not considered "safe" for the new breed of lift-served skiers. The renegade old-timers, typically alpine skiers from the 1950s and 1960s, were determined to preserve the experience of down-mountain skiing that they grew up with. They did not intend to stop skiing powder and interesting snow conditions on remote mountain trails, where they could escape the icy mogul fields of the crowded lift-served mountains.

Frazier Noble, one of the down-mountain skiing holdouts who used to maintain the Pine Hill Trail on Wachusett Mountain, eloquently captured the spirit of backcountry skiing, then and now. He explained to me:

> It's hard to convey to people who haven't done any walking for skiing what the experience is about. It's quite different than just buying an impersonal lift ticket and skiing the mountain from the top. You work hard for the run and get far more exercise than you do when just downhill skiing. The scenery is also an important part of it. These trails were not just a slash down a mountain. They had a lot of interesting natural rolls and turns in them. Also, when you walk up you have time to have long chats with people you're skiing with. That's part of the whole ski experience, too.

Even downhill skiers who were enjoying the convenience of riding chairlifts sensed that something was missing from the experience. Roland Palmedo, who founded Mad River Glen in 1949 and was involved in the early days of the ski area at Stowe, made a plea to skiers not to forget the sport they were leaving behind. Writing in *Appalachia* in 1951, he implored:

> There seems little doubt but that "lift skiing" will continue to be the most popular form of the ski sport....But cross-country touring and the other forms of liftless skiing also have their rewards. The feeling of being on an expedition, the sense of having to cope with whatever lies ahead, the constant change of view or landscape, the companionship of a group moving together, the small adventures of a day on the trail, these things appeal to skiers who have a little of the pioneering instinct, who occasionally like to get off the beaten track, and away from the crowd on the slanted circuit.

Palmedo's words could just as well have been a eulogy for ski touring. The advent of lift-served skiing was the kiss of death—or at least suspended animation—for backcountry skiing. Those who once flocked to the mountains of the North Country to explore new ski routes were now bombing down the ski area slopes of Vermont, New Hampshire, and New York. Skiers of the era recall how the number of people skiing in the backcountry around places like Mount Mansfield dropped from about forty on a typical weekend in the early 1930s to no more than a half-dozen by the mid-1940s.

The evolution in ski equipment exemplified what was happening to the sport of skiing. Rigid downhill boots and bindings that locked the heel down made it impossible to ski uphill or even on flat terrain. The new gear was strictly for going downhill. By the 1950s, the sport of cross-country skiing evolved its own specialized equipment, consisting of lightweight, skinny racing equipment designed for use on prepared, generally flat, ski trails. The split between "downhill" and "cross-country" skiing was made, and the radically different equipment made it impossible to bridge the divide. This division was to grow even wider until the late 1970s.

The down-mountain ski era reflected the social and economic conditions of its time. The nation was emerging from the Great Depression, and the period that followed was one where community, resourcefulness, and bootstrapping were valued. Down-mountain skiing fit right in with this cultural ethos, and it provided economic and social relief for many depressed rural towns. By contrast, the fifties and sixties heralded a time of economic prosperity. Suddenly, sweat equity and camaraderie in the mountains had little cachet. Instead, the nation was seduced by the lure of consumerism, the pursuit of wealth, and fixation on all things "modern." The space race was underway, and being a downhill skier was viewed as a badge of affluence. Backcountry skiing was a relic, a throwback to a bygone era.

People who continued cross-country skiing in the mountains in the 1950s and 1960s were a relatively small and hardy bunch. Joe Pete Wilson, a member of the 1960 Olympic biathlon team who skied in the Green Mountains and the

Skiing the Nose Dive on Mount Mansfield in the 1930s.
Photo courtesy Charlie Lord Collection

Adirondacks, remembers that it was in the mid-1960s, when he was working at a ski resort, that people heard about him and came to ask him about cross-country skiing. He gave a few lessons and answered people's questions. Their curiosity had been piqued when they saw high school and college students out cross-country skiing. There were also many older people who had cross-country skied as kids, or who had parents who skied cross-country. They didn't know what to call the kind of skiing they grew up with. They just thought of it as skiing.

The revival of cross-country skiing was also starting to take place at colleges such as Dartmouth. Dartmouth's downhill ski team and its coach, the late Al Merrill, were nationally renowned. But students noticed that Merrill and a few of his friends "would go out 'touring' after hours," recounted David Hooke in *Reaching That Peak,* a history of the Dartmouth Outing Club (DOC). In 1964, Merrill "was persuaded to give the DOC 'several pointers on ski touring.' By January 1965 ski touring 'was fast becoming the winter's most popular sport.'" In March 1965, a DOC newsletter stated:

> [DOC] managed a surprising number of ski touring trips this winter despite the often filthy snow conditions. Large numbers of men, most of whom traveled on hand-hewn skis garnished with make-shift bindings, glided through weather as diverse as red klister and blue stick. It's a good feeling when your ski sticks on the kick and slides on the glide—an occasional bright eye, raised brow and incredulous mouth numbly muttering "Christ, it works!!!"

A turning point in the revival of cross-country skiing was the sudden availability of inexpensive skis. In the mid-1960s, the first fiberglass downhill skis came on the market. People quickly traded in their old wooden models, which were easily converted into cross-country skis with a little shaving and narrowing to lighten them up. Hooke reports that at Dartmouth, "it is understandable, given the spirit of the times, why touring would have had such appeal: not only was there now a whole lot of obsolete downhill equipment, but converting it and using it would be a great way to get away from 'it all'—meaning lift lines, crowds, and the other trappings of the 'new' Alpine skiing of the day."

In 1970 Joe Pete Wilson and William Lederer co-authored *The Complete Cross-Country Skiing and Ski Touring* (now out of print). It sold briskly—a sign that change was in the air.

The 1970s saw the growth of cross-country skiing at ski-touring centers. But by the late 1970s another small-scale revival began brewing within the world of cross-country skiing. A small group of mountaineers-turned-skiers, cross-country ski instructors, and alpine skiers who had grown bored with the lift-area scene longed to add some adventure to their ski experience. They were getting restless, and touring-center skiing was simply not enough to entertain them anymore. In an effort to combine their mountain climbing with their skiing, they began experimenting with using downhill skiing techniques on cross-country skis. Cross-country skiers began parallel skiing and even revived the defunct telemark turn. Experimentation and brainstorming were at a high pitch among skiers around Stowe and Killington. The audacious and talented Ski to Die Club was soon born in the Adirondacks. The publication of Steve Barnett's now classic *Cross-Country Downhill* in 1978 generated further excitement about expanding the limits of Nordic skiing.

With the renewed interest in backcountry skiing came a concurrent evolution in equipment. The lightweight skis and boots of ski tourers and racers were inadequate for the rigors of backcountry skiing. Karhu and Fischer, both with U.S. headquarters in New England, were two of the first companies to respond to the demand from telemarkers and mountain skiers for a heavy-duty ski. The metal-edged Fischer Europa 77 went on sale in the early 1970s, and the skis that became enduring classics—the Fischer Europa 99 and Karhu XCD-GT—were introduced in 1978. Other manufacturers followed suit, and there is now a wide array of choices available to backcountry skiers.

By the early 1990s, so-called "telemark" skiers were a firmly established skiing subculture. Every ski area in the country now has a small cadre of die-hard free-heel skiers. Telemarkers are borrowing technique and equipment from their alpine brethren and have cobbled together a fresh, eclectic, irreverent sport. Freeheelers have honed their technique to a remarkable degree, skiing virtually everywhere that alpine skiers go. And then they go even further, using the benefit of their Nordic heritage to head off into the high mountains. The 1990s witnessed a full-blown revival of backcountry skiing, as skiers fled the increasingly homogenized experience offered at ski areas in search of something wilder, more authentic.

Snowboarders are the latest snow-sliders to join in the quest for untamed territory. Jake Burton Carpenter began making the first snowboards in 1977 from his workshop in Londonderry, Vermont. He soon convinced Stratton Mountain to allow his innovation on its ski slopes. The rest is history: Snowboarding has boomed, its popularity driven by a young new generation of snow-sliders. By 1996 the number of snowboarders (3.7 million) for the first time surpassed the total number of people who were cross-country skiing in the United States (3.4 million). (In New England, however, there are still twice as many cross-country skiers as snowboarders.)

By the late 1990s, snowboarders were showing up at trailheads, slapping on snowshoes, and disappearing into the high peaks. Now backcountry skiers often come across the distinctive, graceful tracks of a snowboarder. It is a sign of creative ferment.

There has been enormous cross-fertilization between *glisse* enthusiasts in recent years. Alpine boots have become softer and more flexible, telemark boots are now plastic and stiffer, snowboarders are experimenting with split boards (a.k.a. "skis"), and the skinny Nordic skis of yore have been traded in for fatter alpine-style "shaped" skis. This process of experimentation has been going on for more than a century: we are simply searching for ever better ways to travel deep into the winter wilderness.

Skiing has come full circle since the 1930s. Skiers and snowboarders are now in the process of rediscovering the techniques and terrain pioneered by an earlier generation. By discovering the uphill part of snow travel, snowboarders have thrown open the door to a vast mountain landscape. And by reclaiming the downhill component of skiing, Nordic skiers have once again opened up the mountains for exploration on skis. The down-mountain trails have had new life breathed into them—or maybe their old spirit has been revived. This spirit is simply the quest for adventure and a love of the mountains. It has an uncanny way of transcending the barriers of time to bring together everyone who feels its pull.

The Tours

The ski and snowboard tours in this book were chosen because they are "classics." Classic tours in the Northeast have a special character. The mountain ranges in this region are unlike any others in the United States: the elevations are small, but the conditions are distinctly alpine.

There are several qualities that are necessary for a tour to be considered a classic.

History. Many of the tours have historic significance. They were trails that formed the hub of down-mountain skiing activity seventy years ago. Many were built by the Civilian Conservation Corps (CCC) in the 1930s. They represent a slice of Northeastern culture as well as some of the best skiing to be found anywhere. The CCC and other trailblazers in the Northeast had their choice of where the best ski runs would go. The enduring quality and popularity of those trails today are a testament to the keen eye they had for choosing the best routes.

Aesthetics. A classic ski or snowboard tour must have scenic value that captures the spirit of the northeastern mountains and forests, such as picturesque birch forests and accessible mountain summits. A classic tour may travel the full range of northeastern terrain, or it may showcase one aspect of this special landscape.

Quality of Skiing and Snowboarding. Classic tours include high-quality skiing and snowboarding terrain. Quality means variety: The best tours hold your interest because they call upon a full range of techniques. A classic ski tour might include skating on flats, diagonal striding on straightaways, skinning up a mountainside, and telemarking or parallel skiing down an exciting powder run. A classic snowboard tour combines the challenge of an ascent with the fun of negotiating natural terrain features, including streambeds, narrow trails, and the dips and rolls of a mountain. This is total skiing and snowboarding—not specialized subdivisions of these sports.

In short, a classic tour has it all.

DIFFICULTY RATINGS FOR SKIERS

The ski tours in this book are intended for experienced cross-country skiers who are comfortable skiing on a variety of terrain. A skier who is proficient on intermediate trails at a cross-country ski center should be able to ski most of the routes in this book. None of the tours in this book are intended for novice cross-country skiers.

Good downhill skiing opportunities are an important part of most classic ski tours described here. No mountain ski tour is complete without a fun descent. Indeed, the thrill of a long backcountry downhill run has drawn skiers to the mountains for years.

Each tour is rated *moderate*, *more difficult*, or *most difficult*.

Moderate. The terrain includes gentle hills. A good snowplow technique or step turn should suffice for skiing downhill.

More difficult. The terrain includes extended, steeper uphill and downhill sections. Proficiency at making a turn on steeper terrain—using telemark, parallel, snowplow, kick turns, or other techniques—is necessary. Three tours—Woodward Mountain Trail, Bolton-Trapp Trail, and Long Trail/Monroe Skyline—are rated *more difficult +*. The "+" signifies that these tours are particularly remote and/or time consuming (due to tricky route-finding, access, etc.), and skiers should account for this in their trip planning.

Most difficult. The terrain includes sustained downhill skiing on trails that are narrow, steep, or both. The ability to link turns, sometimes quickly, is necessary.

These difficulty ratings are subjective and extremely variable for any given tour. They describe approximately what the trail would be like to ski in average conditions: moderately heavy powder over a solid base that may be broken up by another skier's tracks. But *conditions are everything.* A tour that is considered "moderate" in powder conditions can be ferocious in breakable crust. An "easy" ski tour can at times challenge the best skiers. You must know your ability to ski in various conditions and know when the conditions of a trail exceed your abilities. There is no shame in deciding to walk down a steep, narrow trail that you are not comfortable skiing. In fact, it takes considerable experience to know your limits.

This is a regional rating system. The rating of each tour is relative to the difficulty of other tours in the Northeast. These ratings are not necessarily comparable to ratings found in other guidebooks.

DIFFICULTY RATINGS FOR SNOWBOARDERS

The tours in this book that can be snowboarded are boldface in the table of contents and are also noted in the lead information at the top of the chapter. In general, a tour in which there is a sustained downhill on at least half the total distance is considered suitable for snowboarding. Ideally, a good snowboard tour climbs up and rides down, with little need to change equipment on the descent. Where a tour includes rolling terrain—i.e., it follows primarily flat ground, or goes up and down throughout its length—I have not recommended it for snowboarding, and no snowboarding information appears in the lead information. Snowboarders will generally want to keep to tours that I have rated *more difficult* or *most difficult*. These routes have the most sustained downhill grade.

Backcountry terrain and snow are quite different than what you will find at a ski area. Wild snow includes crud, crust, powder, ice, and corn—often all in the same run. Practice at a ski area by riding in the trees and along the edges of the trail. Search out soft snow and figure out how to tame its infinite forms. The master class comes when you put it all together in the backcountry.

Riders who are comfortable on intermediate trails at a ski area should be able to negotiate trails that are rated more difficult. Trails rated most difficult are for advanced riders who are comfortable on all expert (black diamond) ski area trails. You should begin with easier tours and work up to harder ones in order to get a feel for this rating system.

The mountains, of course, do not conform neatly to these recommendations. Even tours that go mostly downhill are likely to include some flat or uphill sections. Snowboarders must be equipped, mentally and technically, to negotiate every kind of terrain that a mountain tour will present. *It is crucial that you bring equipment to navigate flat and uphill terrain!* If you do not have snowshoes, you will become more intimate with the snow than you ever hoped to be—usually wallowing up to your waist. The ride down is the reward for those who can reach the summit.

I have skied all these routes, not snowboarded them. My description of how each tour will ride is intended as general guidance. I have directed riders toward routes with a sustained downhill pitch, and away from rolling trails. This is admittedly a rough estimation, and your experience with a trail may differ. At worst, you will do more snowshoeing than expected. This book tries to open the door and point the way; the adventure of discovery is yours.

SLOPE INCLINE

The steepness of some routes is occasionally described in terms of the angle of the slope. Most skiers and climbers tend to overestimate slope angles. The most accurate way to determine the steepness of a slope is with an inclinometer. The top-of-the-line compasses made by Suunto and Silva include inclinometers. Life-Link also sells a relatively inexpensive Slope Meter. Becoming proficient in estimating slope angles is especially useful in avalanche hazard assessment, where the difference between a 20-degree slope and 35-degree slope is critical (see the chapter Mountaineering Skills and Avalanches for more on this subject).

In general, 20-degree slopes are considered advanced-intermediate downhill terrain, such as what is encountered on the Wright Peak Ski Trail. Slopes of 30 degrees are advanced downhill terrain. They give pause to the vast majority of Nordic skiers, many of whom resort to traversing and kick-turning to get down a slope of this grade. The summit cone of Mount Marcy and the steepest section of the Teardrop Trail on Mount Mansfield fit this description. Forty-degree slopes are the realm of expert skiers and riders. It takes considerable experience and skill to be comfortable on slopes of this severity, particularly if the grade is sustained. Examples of the latter (not described in this book) include the top of the Tuckerman Ravine headwall (below the Lip) in New Hampshire, some of the summit chutes on Mount Mansfield, and some of the Adirondack slides.

A WORD ABOUT SNOWMOBILES

Occasionally, these tours intersect or coincide for a short distance with snowmobile trails. There is often considerable antagonism between skiers and snowmobilers, and I am afraid that skiers must bear an equal share of the blame for whatever bad feelings exist. Skiers do not own the mountains. Snowmobilers have as much right to enjoy the outdoors on their designated trails as skiers do on ski routes. Furthermore, skiers often depend on the kindness of snowmobilers when an evacuation becomes necessary. I have seen snowmobilers provide help during an emergency, often at great inconvenience to themselves.

Skiers should declare peace. A friendly smile or wave to snowmobilers when you are on one of their trails will help restore some sense of mutual respect and civility to these encounters in the woods. It will also keep you from getting run over.

Backcountry Snowboarding

Snowboarders are heeding the same call of the wild that has lured skiers into the outback for many years. Riders come with new tools and a fresh outlook. The high and wild places of the Northeast are a great home for these snow-sliders.

When snowboarding first became popular in the 1980s, the sport was largely confined to ski areas. After all, riders were "gravity slaves": it seemed impossible that they could go anywhere but downhill. Skiers, especially backcountry enthusiasts, dismissed snowboards as "toys" rather than "tools." All that has changed.

Snowboarders are striking out in search of wilder snow. Western riders have been exploring the outback for years. Eastern riders, like skiers of this region, often have not realized how much great backcountry skiing and riding terrain exists here. This guidebook uncovers the limitless backcountry riding possibilities that abound in the Northeastern mountains.

The pioneers of backcountry snowboarding have borrowed freely from all the winter sports to make it possible to travel in the wilderness. They have taken crampons from climbing, poles from skiing, and snowshoes from hikers to get where they want to go. They are even splitting snowboards in two, converting them to temporary skis, in an effort to make one tool do two things. It is a time of great excitement, as snowboarders individually and collectively improvise ways to trample old limitations and expand the boundaries of their sport. Where riders have led, equipment companies are following. Innovative new gear now allows snowboarders to travel uphill and across the flats.

Knowing how to navigate and take care of yourself in the mountains is essential for backcountry boarding. Regardless of whether you are on skis or snowboards, traveling in the backcountry requires preparation. All of the information in this book about clothing, mountaineering skills, and first aid applies equally to snowboarders, skiers, and snowshoers.

Following is information that riders need to use this guide and to tour in the Northeastern backcountry.

BACKCOUNTRY SNOWBOARD EQUIPMENT
BASICS: BOOTS, BOARD, BINDINGS

The basic equipment for snowboarding is evolving and changing so rapidly that any equipment models recommended today will inevitably be outdated tomorrow. A few general considerations should guide your choice of basic equipment.

Comfort is king. You will be wearing whatever you bring into the backcountry for most of the day. Your boots, in particular, should be comfortable for walking, climbing, and riding. There are advantages and drawbacks to both soft and hard boots: Soft boots are very comfortable for snowshoeing and hiking uphill on moderate terrain and riding on soft snow, but they are almost useless for kicking steps in hard snow when climbing a steep gully. Hard boots offer exceptional downhill control and can be used with crampons, but they are heavy and clunky

Snowboarding the summit cone of Mount Marcy, New York's highest peak.

going uphill (hard boots work well with split boards, however, since the binding allows the heel to lift). The bottom line is that both styles, provided they fit comfortably, will work.

Gear to go everywhere. In a typical mountain tour, you will encounter every kind of snow condition. Powder, crud, crust, and ice are all part of the wilderness scene. Choose a snowboard that does it all. Softer freeride, or all-mountain, boards are best. Boards with a nice balanced flex will respond most predictably in unpredictable snow.

Simple is better. A basic tenet of backcountry travel is that everything that can break, will break. Bring gear that is easily repairable in the field. Strap-on bindings are more easily jury-rigged if a strap breaks. Step-in bindings have specialized parts on both the boot and board that may be irreparable in the field. For both bindings, carry spare parts, or even a replacement binding that you can slap on in a hurry.

TOURING GEAR

On many tours, you will spend most of your day going uphill. Following is the equipment that makes it possible to defy gravity.

Snowshoes. Snowshoes are basic equipment for backcountry snowboarding. What skins are to skiers, snowshoes are to boarders: It's the only way to get up the mountain. Look for lightweight, compact snowshoes with bindings that will fit around your snowboard boots. Snowshoes should have a crampon underfoot to climb on hard snow. Avoid the old wooden snowshoes. They are heavy, difficult to pack, and more prone to break.

Poles. Poles often will enable you to get across a flat area without having to take off your board. They are also useful for snowshoeing. Look for collapsible poles that can fit in your pack. Three-section poles collapse the most, and some sectional poles can double as avalanche probes.

Packs. A sturdy day pack is an investment that will last you for many miles and many years. A good winter day pack should have a capacity of 2,000 to 2,500 cubic inches. Look for one of the many models that has an attachment to carry a snowboard and snowshoes.

Wax. The wide surface area of a snowboard makes them prone to drag (i.e., go slowly) in snow. Rub some fluorinated wax on your board. You'll appreciate the glide on long flat run-outs.

Crampons. If your passion is to climb up and ride down the steepest gullies, slides, and trails, crampons are a must. They will make the steep climbs easier and safer. Look for lightweight crampons designed especially for use with soft snowboard boots.

Split boards. Split boards have become popular among backcountry riders in the West. The snowboard is split down the middle and attaches together with metal clamps. Use your board in the two-plank mode (a.k.a. skis) with skins for the climb, then fasten them together into a single snowboard for the descent. This is specialized touring equipment, but if you plan to do a lot of backcountry riding, it is the lightest and easiest way to go.

Repair gear. There is nothing worse than being five miles out on a remote tour and looking down at a broken binding. I know because I've been there. With the mercury plunging, night approaching, and no quick way down, things can get ugly fast. And your gear *will* break. Bring parts to fix your mangled equipment. Anticipate what can break, and be able to fix it. A basic snowboard repair kit should include binding parts (including replacement screws and straps), rope or cord, glue, knife, and a #3 Phillips screwdriver. See the chapter Clothing and Ski Equipment for additional suggestions on repair items. And check the chapter First Aid for what to bring in a first-aid kit.

ATTITUDE

You earn your turns in the backcountry. Do yourself and other skiers and riders a favor by respecting some time-honored trail customs.

Don't posthole the trail! A trail with crotch-deep craters in it is a nasty ride, especially after the holes freeze. Tread softly. Work less. Climb with snowshoes.

Practice powder preservation. Make one snowshoe track instead of packing down the full width of the trail. If possible, snowshoe up the side of the trail so that most of it is left untracked. Take a different trail up than the one you ride down, if you can.

Easy does it. The backcountry is not a ski area. There is no ski patrol, and help will be a long time coming if you need it. Save the sick air and Mach speed for the resort, where your buddies can see you. Ride conservatively in the backcountry, as if getting hurt were not an option. Because it's not.

Learn the mountains. Outdoor skills are even more important than your half-pipe technique out here. Become mountain savvy: Learn about mountain navigation, winter camping, the environment, and avalanches. Take a course, read a book (see the chapter Mountaineering Skills and Avalanches), learn from friends. The more you know, the farther you can go.

Ride friendly. You don't often meet people in the backcountry. When you do, stop and give them room. There's no "right of way" out here—just folks like you who are out to have fun. They'll probably be surprised to see snowboarders. Here's your chance to tell them what it's like to ride where they ski or hike.

Keep it clean. Leave no trace of your passage other than your tracks. Carry out all trash, including cigarette butts.

Help Yourself. Bring extra food, water, clothes, a lighter, and a space blanket. Just in case things don't go as planned.

Have fun. It's why we go.

The Northeastern Ski Season

There is usually good snow cover for skiing in the backcountry of the Northeast from mid-December through early April. In many years, skiing begins by Thanksgiving. Likewise, April snowstorms are not uncommon and are sometimes substantial. December and February are the months with the heaviest snowfall in the northern states, with the snow reaching its greatest depth in late February and early March.

Spring skiing in the Northeast begins in early April. Mount Washington in New Hampshire is the favorite location, where skiing Tuckerman Ravine often continues through June (for a definitive guide to skiing and boarding in Tuckerman Ravine and elsewhere, see *Backcountry Skiing Adventures: Classic Ski and Snowboard Tours in Maine and New Hampshire*, by David Goodman). There is also spring skiing on most of the higher elevation tours in this book, including Mount Mansfield, Mount Marcy, the Wright Peak Ski Trail, Camel's Hump, Big Jay, Avalanche Pass, and the Woodward Mountain Trail.

THE NORTHEASTERN WINTER ENVIRONMENT

Winters in the Northeast are characterized by very cold and wet weather. Cold temperatures are intensified in the mountains, where wind exposure is greatest. Data from the weather observatory on Mount Washington in New Hampshire illustrates this point.

The summit of Mount Washington (6,288 feet) is under cloud cover about 55 percent of the time. The average winter temperature is 15 degrees Fahrenheit; the record low temperature is -46 degrees. Average winds in the winter are 44 MPH and winds greater than 100 MPH have been recorded every month of the year. These are admittedly the most extreme conditions in the East, but it is better to be prepared for the most severe mountain weather than to be caught off guard in the winter.

Table 1 on page 22 presents a climatological profile of the Northeast in the winter.

WINTER WEATHER IN THE NORTHEAST

Location	Mean Snow, Sleet Totals (inches)					Mean Temperature (degrees F)				
	Dec.	Jan.	Feb.	Mar.	Apr.	Dec.	Jan.	Feb.	Mar.	Apr.
Lake Placid, NY*	20.0	21.4	18.5	18.1	18.2	21.1	15.2	18.2	27.2	39.3
Montpelier, VT	23.8	18.2	23.2	17.4	5.0	20.5	15.1	17.5	27.0	40.4
Mount Mansfield, VT+	41.6	36.6	27.8	36.0	24.0	11.1	6.7	11.5	18.0	34.0
Pinkham Notch, NH	35.5	31.4	38.2	34.2	16.0	19.9	15.8	17.3	25.6	37.4
Mount Washington, NH	42.5	39.0	40.5	41.8	29.2	9.3	4.8	5.5	12.0	22.5
Woodstock, NH	23.6	21.2	24.2	17.4	3.09	23.5	18.8	21.3	30.4	42.3
Bar Harbor, ME	14.1	16.1	19.5	12.8	2.6	28.2	23.8	24.6	32.5	42.8
Ripogenus Dam, ME (Baxter State Park)	28.2	25.7	26.8	20.9	7.4	17.7	11.9	13.3	23.6	36.6

Source: National Oceanic and Atmospheric Administration, Climatology of the United States, No. 60, 1951–1973. This is most recent data available.

* Source: Northeast Regional Climate Center Data, 1971–2000.

+ Source: Mount Mansfield weather station, 1982–1987.

TABLE 1

Clothing and Ski Equipment

There is no one right set of clothes or equipment that works for every person. There are, however, some basic guidelines that should be taken into consideration when you are looking for new gear.

DRESSING TO STAY WARM

Clothing for backcountry skiing and riding must keep you warm and relatively dry. Cotton is notoriously unable to do this. When cotton gets wet, it acts like a towel, getting wetter and wetter and drawing out precious body heat and energy.

The best clothes to wear in the winter are those made of synthetics such as polypropylene, polyester, and nylon. These types of clothing are sold under various names, including Capilene, CoolMax, Thermax, and Polarfleece. All these fabrics are similar in that they retain very little moisture and dry from the inside out when they get wet. The body heat of an active skier or rider is usually adequate to dry them.

The most effective way to dress to stay warm in winter is to wear a number of lighter layers rather than one bulky layer. This technique is called layering. What keeps you warm is the air trapped next to your body, not clothing. By wearing a number of loose, lighter layers, you can most efficiently trap air, which is warmed by your body.

For layering to be effective, you must shed a layer before you begin sweating profusely. Heavy perspiration in the winter can be dangerous. It can lead to dehydration and will saturate your clothes just as if you were standing in the rain.

A typical layering system for an active day of skiing is a polypropylene shirt, a fleece sweater, lightweight fleece pants, and a windbreaker of nylon or Gore-Tex. In your backpack would be a heavier fleece or pile jacket, nylon or Gore-Tex overpants, and a compact down (or equivalent) parka.

Wind protection is especially important in the northeastern mountains. All the sweaters in your closet won't keep you warm with a 30 MPH wind slicing through them. A parka or anorak made of a tightly woven and fast-drying fabric such as Gore-Tex is an essential part of any layering system. As your outer layer, this shell should also be water resistant. Wet snows are common in the Northeast, and don't be surprised if you encounter rain as well.

A common mistake skiers and riders make when dressing is to throw on a down parka and head up the mountain. In my experience, the temperature would have to be well below zero to be comfortable skiing in a down parka. It is simply too much insulation for an aerobic activity like skiing. A good practice is to start skiing while feeling a bit chilled. You will warm up within a few minutes and save having to undress and repack a few hundred yards down the trail.

THE RIGHT SKIS FOR THE JOB*

Seventy years ago there was only one type of ski. You couldn't really go wrong: You used the same ski for cross-country, ski jumping, and downhill skiing. Today, selecting a ski involves wading through a dizzying forest of specialized gear. There are now different skis for skating, touring on groomed trails, touring off-trail, racing, jumping, lift-area skiing, backcountry telemarking, and alpine touring.

The best skiers can ski most routes on any equipment. That isn't to say it is easy to take skinny cross-country skis down Mount Mansfield. It's just that high-tech equipment is no substitute for good technique and commitment. Indeed, most of the ski routes in this book were first skied on seven-foot-long hickory skis with cable bindings. Early skiers simply used what they had. Their passion, boldness, and creativity were far more important catalysts for their mountain explorations than what was under their feet.

Having said that, your choice of ski equipment *does* matter. Gear has become absurdly specialized, so much so that it is quite possible to buy equipment that is completely inappropriate for backcountry terrain. The easier backcountry tours can be done in light cross-country gear. But you would find most routes much easier to ski and more enjoyable with equipment that is better suited to a wide range of conditions.

What is the ideal backcountry ski setup? For me, it would be a superlight boot that is fleet on the flats but stiff and solid on the descents, mated with a superlight but indestructible binding, mounted on a superlight ski that is as comfortable flat-tracking as it is busting through crud and descending a steep gully.

Needless to say, this ideal marriage of light weight and bombproof stability doesn't exist yet. Thus, choosing a ski requires making compromises. No one ski or boot does everything well. Err on the side of what you do most and where you want to go. Lightweight gear is the choice for light touring or rolling terrain, while heavier equipment is the choice for steeper terrain and more difficult conditions.

Following are some general suggestions on what to look for in equipment. This discussion is limited to Nordic-style backcountry ski equipment. For recommendations on the latest ski models, and for information on alpine-touring (randonée) equipment, see the equipment reviews in magazines such as *Back Country* and *Couloir*.

* See the Backcountry Snowboarding chapter for information on snowboard equipment.

Boots

Good backcountry boots are the most important investment you will make. The reasons are simple: comfort and control. You will likely be in your ski boots for most of the day. Comfort is king in boot selection: If your feet are comfortable, you will be happy. If your feet hurt, no amount of pretty scenery will arrest your misery. Boots also make a critical difference in your ability to control your skis. If you are upgrading your equipment piecemeal, it makes sense to buy boots first.

Good backcountry ski boots have a more rigid, higher-ankle profile than conventional cross-country ski boots. Their key attribute is that they are torsionally stiff. This means that when you twist your leg to turn the ski, the twisting motion is transferred directly into turning power on the ski, instead of into just flexing the boot. You are probably familiar with the terrifying sensation of flying downhill on cross-country skis with old boots that twist uselessly in the bindings. A good, stiff boot will add an element of control to your skiing you may never have experienced before.

Leather or plastic boots? Both materials work well, and each has its strengths. Leather boots are very comfortable. Many people have a favorite pair of trusty old leather boots that they have enjoyed touring in for years. The most versatile new leather boots incorporate elements from plastic boots. Having one or two buckles can greatly enhance your control on the downhills, and can do wonders to keep an aging leather boot snug around your foot.

The newest plastic boots are remarkably comfortable. They require little maintenance, stay dry, and have unmatched downhill performance. Take extra care in fitting yourself in plastic boots. One brand may fit your foot, and another may not. You can fine-tune most fit problems at an alpine ski shop that has experience with adjusting plastic boots.

You may want to consider buying double boots if you have chronic problems with cold feet. Double boots are heavy but warm. Single boots with insulated supergaiters are another possible solution. (See the section on frostbite in the chapter First Aid for more on this.)

Avoid buying too much boot. A clunky, heavy boot will make climbing and touring on the flats feel like a tiresome trudge. If the majority of your skiing is on moderate terrain, opt for a lighter backcountry boot rather than a boot that is oriented to lift-serviced skiing. Skip the ultrastiff telemark racing boots. The high collars that reach nearly to your knee will cause you nothing but pain on uphill climbs and long tours. They are strictly for lift-served skiing.

Unless you can find a pair of used boots, be prepared to pay a relatively hefty price for good boots. They are expensive, but it is an investment that should last many years.

Skis

The tours in this book with sections of extended downhill skiing that are rated *more difficult* or *most difficult* are most easily done by the majority of skiers on heavier backcountry skis—commonly called telemark skis. Telemark skis are heavy-duty, metal-edged skis designed for maximum control on variable, difficult terrain. They are wider than most touring skis, enabling them to float better in powder and to provide a more stable platform when you are wearing a pack and skiing on uneven ground. Metal edges are particularly useful in the East, where ice is a fact of life for the backcountry skier. Telemark skis with measurements of 85mm or more at the tip are especially user-friendly in soft snow and on more challenging tours. It is much easier to ski in crud, powder, and heavy snow on a wider board.

Metal-edged skis do have a drawback: They are heavy and consequently not as enjoyable to ski with on flatter terrain or long tours. Metal-edged skis are unnecessary for skiing in powder or on flat terrain where control on downhills is not a primary consideration.

Ski tours rated *moderate* in this book generally can be skied comfortably on edgeless touring skis, provided you have sturdy boots and reasonably good snow conditions. A good backcountry touring ski should be fairly wide for flotation in deep snow, have ample sidecut to facilitate turning, and be solidly constructed.

Camber refers to the arch in the middle of the ski; the space created by this arch is called the wax pocket. A double-camber ski has a stiff arch, while a single-camber ski has little or no arch. Double-camber skis are especially nice for moderate touring, since they hold wax better over the course of a long tour. Single-camber skis offer more control at high speeds and are especially suited to lift-serviced skiing and more challenging backcountry tours. Single-camber skis can be waxed (the wax may wear off a little faster than on double-camber skis) or used with climbing skins. In general, choose a single-camber ski if you ski primarily at lift areas and on routes rated *more difficult* and *most difficult*. Opt for a double-camber touring ski if you prefer the more moderate tours.

The debate over which is better, waxless or waxable skis, should really not be so strident. Waxing skis is not that complicated, and it is made even simpler with the two-wax systems that are available (one wax for new snow, another wax for old snow). The tricks of waxing can be learned from other skiers, or by simple trial and error. Waxable skis are faster, quieter, and better climbers than waxless skis. Simply put, a fast ski is a fun ski to tour on. However, if you favor moderate tours, ski only occasionally, do a lot of spring skiing, or if you just don't want to be bothered with waxing, modern waxless skis do a fine job.

Bindings

Heavy-duty three-pin or cable bindings are the best choice for backcountry skiing. Bindings designed for telemarking are made of strong metal alloys that can take considerable abuse. They are much sturdier and offer greater control than light-weight touring bindings. Getting stranded with a mangled lightweight binding when you are five miles from nowhere should convince you that heavy-duty bind-ings are worth the extra investment.

The so-called "backcountry" step-in boot-binding systems made by Salomon and Rottefella are fine for moderate touring. For more challenging tours, they do not offer the same level of control and durability as a cable or three-pin binding, and are nearly impossible to repair if they break.

POLES

Adjustable poles are a good choice for backcountry skiing. These poles can col-lapse or extend, depending on the demands of the terrain; they can be kept long for the uphill climb and shortened for downhill skiing. However, adjustable poles can be exasperating, collapsing when you don't want them to and refusing to adjust. Two-section poles are simpler and less likely to collapse unexpectedly than three-section poles.

If you travel in steep terrain, you should invest in probe poles. These can be joined together to form one long avalanche probe, a useful feature when skiing in slide-prone areas. Note that not all adjustable poles convert to avalanche probes; check to be sure that your poles can join together.

CLIMBING SKINS

Climbing skins are essential on most of these ski tours. Climbing skins are ski-length strips of fabric with unidirectional hairs. These hairs mat down when ski-ing forward and grip the snow, preventing the ski from sliding backward. The best skins are made out of nylon or mohair. They mimic the action of animal skins, which were actually pelts that early skiers strapped to the bottom of their skis in order to ski uphill.

Skiers will often spend at least a half-day skiing up a steep mountain trail to reach a summit. On many of these routes, the ascent would become so tiring and frustrating without skins that most skiers would understandably abandon their destination. Think of skins as a safety item: They permit you to ration your ener-gy efficiently and avoid exhaustion. Being able to gain purchase in any type of snow also enables you to get out quickly if the need arises. Skins can be left on for narrow downhill sections that you find particularly desperate. They will slow you down considerably, but they also make it difficult to turn.

Skins require some care. They should be dried out after each use, folded back together, and stored in a dry place. Adhesive skins require a reapplication of glue every season or two.

Nylon and mohair skins work equally well. Nylon tends to be more durable and dries quicker, while mohair glides better. Look for adhesive skins that are wide enough to cover the bases of your skis; a tail hook is a nice feature too. Kicker skins—which cover only about half the ski length—also work well on more moderate terrain. Avoid plastic skins. They are cheaper, but they have virtually no forward glide and the attachment straps tend to roll over the edges of the ski when skiing on a sidehill.

PACKS

Look for a heavy-duty day pack that is designed to carry skis. Jury-rigged ski attachments can be a constant aggravation. The pack should have a capacity of 2,000 to 2,500 cubic inches. A sternum strap is crucial to stabilize the load when skiing downhill, and a well-padded waist belt makes all the difference in comfort. Cheap packs fall apart. Invest in a good pack, and it will last for years.

MISCELLANEOUS

If you are an avid telemarker, you should invest in **kneepads**. Injuries ranging from bruised to broken kneecaps have become increasingly common among telemarkers, but they can usually be prevented by placing a little foam and plastic between you and the ground. The best protection is the style of kneepads used for skateboarding or in-line skating: They have a molded plastic cup over a layer of closed-cell foam and are available at ski and skate shops. You can also find them in building supply stores (they are used by carpenters).

Eye protection is essential for skiing through trees or on hiking trails. Ski goggles, glacier glasses, sunglasses, or sport shades will all do the job.

Consider carrying a compact **sleeping bag** on more remote day trips. Having a sleeping bag along is a wise safety precaution, particularly if your party is large or includes some inexperienced skiers.

BACKCOUNTRY REPAIR

Your equipment *will* break. Backcountry skiing is abusive. Skis snap, bindings rip out, poles turn into pretzels, boot pinholes blow out, and packs detonate at the seams. About the only thing that you can count on is that each of these mishaps will occur at the least convenient moment.

Backcountry skiers should be equipped to perform functional field repairs. Below are basic items needed for a repair kit.

Screwdriver. A #3 Phillips screwdriver fits cross-country binding screws. Several handy palm-size drivers are available from ski shops, or you can just buy a stubby screwdriver at a hardware store.

Glue. Quick-drying Super-Glue works well for everything from securing binding screws to reinforcing a broken ski. Pack it securely—it can leak in your pack.

Hose clamps. A small assortment of hose clamps is useful for quickly repairing broken poles and skis. Have some small enough to fit around a pole, and some large enough to fit around overlapping broken ski ends.

Aluminum flashing. Aluminum flashing can be used to splint a broken or bent pole or ski. For a pole, wrap a section around the break and hold it in place with hose clamps. Skis can be patched similarly, although it is a more tenuous splint. Curved snow stakes for tents are also very useful for splinting poles.

Screws. Binding screws love to loosen. The best solution is prevention. Put a dab of Shoe-Goo or silicone caulk in the screw holes and under the binding before mounting the binding on the ski. Get into the habit of checking your bindings before each outing to make sure the screws are tight. Always have on hand a small assortment of screws. Extra binding screws can be obtained from a ski shop. A few oversized screws are useful in case a binding hole becomes stripped.

Steel wool. Steel wool can be mixed into glue to fill stripped binding screw holes. It hardens like a steel casing around the screw.

Nylon cord. Carry at least ten feet of it—it is invaluable in binding repair. It can be used to replace a lost bail, or rigged like a cable binding.

Knife or multi-tool. Swiss army knives are useful for spreading peanut butter and for doing just about anything else you can imagine. The multi-tools that include pliers, screwdrivers, wire cutters, and a knife are especially useful.

Extra binding. At zero degrees with night approaching, you'll appreciate not having to improvise a binding repair that may not even work. Keep an extra ski binding in the bottom of your pack (ski shops may have an orphaned binding kicking around that they are willing to part with). Use the awl on your Swiss army knife to start a new screw hole if you have to.

Duct tape. When all else fails, so will the duct tape. But have it along anyway. A good way to carry it is to wrap a wad around your poles. And keep a roll in your car to replenish your supply. It's always useful for something.

BACKCOUNTRY SKIING & SNOWBOARDING CHECKLIST

CLOTHING

- ❏ Hat and neck gaiter (fleece or wool)
- ❏ Gaiters
- ❏ Weatherproof gloves/mitts
- ❏ Synthetic or wool socks
- ❏ Synthetic long underwear
- ❏ Lightweight fleece sweater
- ❏ Heavyweight fleece or pile jacket and/or vest
- ❏ Compact down parka (optional)
- ❏ Gore-Tex* overpants
- ❏ Gore-Tex* parka with hood

* or equivalent waterproof/breathable material

BASIC EQUIPMENT

- ❏ Heavy-duty backcountry skis or snowboard
- ❏ Backcountry ski or snowboard boots
- ❏ Adjustable poles (preferably avalanche probes)
- ❏ Day pack (approximately 2,500 cubic inches)
- ❏ Climbing skins (for skiers)

- ❏ Kneepads (for telemarkers)
- ❏ Eye protection (goggles, glacier glasses, sport shades)
- ❏ First aid kit (including blister treatment and assortment of bandages—see text)
- ❏ Ski or snowboard repair kit (including screwdriver and pliers—see text)
- ❏ Extra ski or snowboard binding
- ❏ Headlamp
- ❏ Compass
- ❏ Topographic map
- ❏ Waterproof matches
- ❏ Wide-mouth insulated water bottle and water
- ❏ Extra food
- ❏ Sunscreen and lip protection
- ❏ Ski wax and scraper
- ❏ Knife or multi-tool
- ❏ Plastic garbage bags (for carrying out trash and protecting extra clothes from weather)

Mountaineering Skills and Avalanches

Backcountry skiing and snowboarding are just forms of winter mountaineering—hence the term *ski mountaineering*, which aptly describes most of the tours in this book. Skiers and snowboarders need good mountaineering skills to travel safely in the winter wilderness. "Good ski technique," as Steve Barnett writes in *The Best Ski Touring in America*, "rates well behind avalanche knowledge, navigational skills, and camping skills as something you need to know to ski." Some of these skills can be learned from books or classes. Others, like good judgment, must be honed by experience.

This book will not attempt to teach mountaineering or ski technique in any depth, since other books and courses cover these subjects thoroughly. For an excellent introduction to winter skills, consider taking the annual winter mountaineering course offered jointly by the AMC and the Adirondack Mountain Club (see appendix A for contact information for these and other outdoor organizations). To sharpen you book knowledge of mountain travel, the bible on this subject is *Mountaineering: The Freedom of the Hills,* published by The Mountaineers (see appendix B, "Recommended Reading"). However, the skills in which every backcountry skier and snowboarder should be proficient are briefly described below.

MOUNTAINEERING JUDGMENT

Most judgment calls in the mountains ultimately come down to a decision about how wide a margin of safety you leave yourself. In the winter, mountaineers need a greater margin of safety than in the summer. An unplanned night out in the snow without adequate equipment can have serious consequences.

Good judgment in the mountains requires taking into consideration a range of variables. Among other things, you must consider the strength of each individual in your party (Are they strong skiers? Are they in good physical condition?); the condition of each person at the point a decision is being made (Is everybody warm? Is anybody nearing exhaustion?); the objective hazards your party will encounter (How exposed is the route to the elements? Is there avalanche danger? What is the weather forecast? What are the snow conditions?); and what you are equipped to accomplish.

Anticipation is critical in the mountains. The more you are prepared for the unlikely, the greater your margin of safety. If you choose to play things close to

Sign warning skiers of avalanche risk on the way to Mount Marcy and the Adirondack High Peaks.

your limit, you should be prepared for the consequences of the inevitable time when things don't go the way you had planned.

NAVIGATION

Trails can be especially difficult to follow in winter. Blazes on summer hiking trails are often obscured by snow or are difficult to see, particularly during snowstorms. Whiteouts are particularly disorienting on exposed mountain summits. It is essential, therefore, that skiers be proficient with a map and compass, and carry both of them in the backcountry. A global positioning system (GPS) and altimeter can also be useful for establishing your location, but these are only adjuncts to good map-reading skills.

Maps are the most important items for navigation. Ideally, if you are closely following a map, the compass should rarely have to come out. The two most common types of trail maps are *sketch maps* and *topographic maps*. Sketch maps show the rough outline of trails in an area. They are often not drawn to an accurate scale, may not indicate direction, and do not show changes in elevation. They are useful in combination with topographic maps to determine the approximate location of trails.

A topographic map provides detailed information about the landscape. It is the basic tool of the backcountry traveler. Learning to read topographic maps takes time, but developing a fundamental grasp of how they work is not difficult. Simply put, each contour line represents a change in elevation. The most common contour intervals used on maps published by the U.S. Geological Survey (USGS) are 10, 20, 40, and 100 feet. Some northeastern maps, including many that cover the Adirondacks, have been issued with metric contour intervals. This information is printed at the bottom of each USGS map.

Topographic maps are extremely helpful when planning a ski or snowboard route because you can tailor the tour to the type of terrain you are seeking. Areas with contour lines bunched tightly together indicate steep slopes, while wider spaces between the lines indicate a more moderate grade. You will get a feel for what type of topography to look for on maps by checking a map when you are skiing and seeing how the terrain is depicted.

The best way to stay oriented with a map is to check it frequently, especially when you arrive at obvious landmarks. This means keeping the map accessible at all times. If you have to dig in your pack to get it, chances are you won't bother until it is too late. Use the map to predict what is around the next bend and what you will encounter in the next half-mile. If the terrain is not what you predicted it would be, you have either miscalculated the distance or are in the wrong place. Either way, you have been alerted to the problem sooner rather than later and can make a quick adjustment.

Maps come in different scales. Most USGS maps that cover the Northeast now come in the 7.5-minute series, which cover an area of about 6 by 9 miles. These maps have a scale of 1:24,000, where 2.6 inches equals 1 mile.

Map reading in the Northeast can be tricky. Mountaineers accustomed to navigating in big western ranges can easily become confused by the small scale of eastern terrain. Distant landmarks are often impossible to sight from the forested trails, and small drainages on the map can be indistinct. The key here is to pay attention to subtle changes in the terrain and to look around frequently to see how you are oriented to distant landmarks. Navigating here is like skiing here: our compact landscape makes everything a little more challenging.

A compass is a hand-held plastic device with a floating magnetic needle inside that points north—almost. The needle actually points to magnetic north, and the angle of deviation from true north must be corrected depending on where you are on the planet. In the Northeast, magnetic declination ranges from 14 degrees west in the Adirondacks and Vermont, to 20 degrees west in northern Maine. The exact declination for a given area will be printed on your topographic map. This means that if you take a bearing from a map, you should add the amount of declination for that area in order to arrive at an accurate bearing to follow. (If you tend to forget whether to add or subtract in the Northeast, think *add*-iron-dacks.) If you take a bearing from a distant landmark like a mountain summit, you must subtract the declination before using the compass bearing on a map. This compensates for the amount that the needle is exaggerating the angle between you and the distant object due to its affinity for magnetic north.

Compasses can be used to establish whether or not you are going in the right direction, to pinpoint your position (by triangulation), or to follow a bearing. The latter is especially useful in dense eastern forests, where following a bearing is sometimes the only way to bushwhack your way out of the deep woods if you've gotten turned around. Remember that compasses are not the only indicators of direction of travel. You can always use the sun: It rises in the east, spends most of its day in the south, and sets in the west. If you've really gotten waylaid, remember that the moon also rises in the east, and the North Star points north.

WINTER CAMPING

Knowing how to comfortably spend a night outdoors in the winter opens up exciting new possibilities for backcountry travelers. Multiday ski tours can be planned to visit the most remote areas of wilderness. It is also important for skiers to know how to spend a night safely in winter in the event you are unexpectedly benighted.

Many of the principles of dressing to stay warm apply to sleeping warm. The key is to generate and preserve as much body heat as possible. This may be done in several ways.

The basic equipment for preserving body heat while sleeping is a sleeping bag and an insulating ground pad. A sleeping bag keeps you warm by trapping air next to your skin. The more loft, or trapped air, a sleeping bag has, the warmer it is. A winter sleeping bag should keep you warm down to about zero degrees Fahrenheit. Both down and synthetic (such as Polarguard and Quallofil) sleeping bags are appropriate, although down bag users must take care to keep their bags dry. If you do not own a winter sleeping bag, two lighter bags, with one inside the other, should be sufficient.

A good sleeping bag is useless in the snow without insulation beneath it. Air mattresses, such as a Therm-A-Rest, or pads made of closed-cell foam do a good job of insulating you from the snow. The more space between you and the snow, the warmer you will be. In addition to using your sleeping pad, consider sleeping on extra clothes, on an extra sleeping pad, or on your pack. Also, be sure that your sleeping pad is rated to withstand temperatures below zero. Summer pads, although they look the same, will crack at low temperatures.

Winter mountaineers should know how to construct an emergency snow shelter. Snow has remarkable insulating properties. That is one of the reasons hibernating animals can stay alive when they dig into the snow for the winter. If you get benighted without adequate equipment, digging a snow cave may save your life or your extremities. The temperature inside a snow cave can easily be 30 degrees warmer than the outside air. There are many types of snow shelters that work. Find a book that discusses snow shelters (see appendix B, Recommended Reading, at the back of this book), and spend a day playing with a shovel in your backyard to try your hand at building several different types of shelters.

Even with a good sleeping bag, your body will need enough caloric fuel to generate heat throughout the night. The best fuel is high-carbohydrate foods such as pasta, which should be eaten in quantity before going to bed. In addition, keep a bag of quick-acting, high-energy food such as trail mix next to you as you sleep. If you get cold during the night, eating a few handfuls of trail mix may be all you need to keep your furnace burning.

AVALANCHE AWARENESS

Avalanches pose a serious danger to skiers and snowboarders. The fact that the Northeast does not have a *lot* of avalanches should not be confused with the notion that it does not have *any*. Fortunately, the Northeast has less of the type of terrain and snow conditions that favor avalanches, but it does have its share. And an avalanche in the Northeast is as deadly as an avalanche in Colorado.

Snow Ranger Brad Ray of the White Mountain National Forest in New Hampshire estimates that twenty to twenty-five potentially deadly avalanches rake the flanks of Mount Washington in New Hampshire each winter, although most of them release when no one is around. There have been many tragic exceptions: In 1996, two skiers died in an avalanche in the Gulf of Slides and a hiker was killed in an avalanche on Lion's Head on Mount Washington. In February 2000, another skier was killed in Gulf of Slides, and a group of five skiers in the Adirondacks was caught in a massive avalanche; one skier died, and another was severely injured. In March 2000, two skiers died in avalanches in the Chic Chocs Mountains in Quebec in separate incidents.

The danger of avalanches is greatest on slopes of 30 to 45 degrees. *This danger is at its peak during a snowstorm and in the first twenty-four hours afterward.* Wind-loaded slopes and gullies also can be very unstable even when there is low avalanche danger elsewhere. A new cornice at the top of a slope is one indication that it has been wind-loaded; avoid these slopes for several days until they settle.

Any ravines, gullies, slides, or steep, open slopes that you might be skiing can avalanche when the necessary combination of conditions exists. If you ski on steep, open terrain, you should carry standard avalanche safety equipment. This includes a shovel, avalanche transceiver (you must have a newer 457 kHz model), and probe poles. But carrying rescue gear does not confer immunity: Once you have to resort to locating a buried friend with a beacon, you've already blown it.

The key to traveling in avalanche-prone terrain is *prevention*. Records show that most avalanche victims trigger the fatal slide themselves. *When in doubt, back off.* It simply is not worth it to jump onto a suspect slope. And just because some-

Digging a snow pit to check the avalanche danger on Mount Katahdin, Maine.

one else skied a slope does not prove that it is stable. Passing up a tempting powder run takes considerable experience and wisdom.

Assess the snow conditions when you are skiing in avalanche country. First, open your eyes and look around: Note signs of instability on surrounding slopes (cracks, sloughs, settling underfoot). Nearby avalanche activity or debris is a major warning sign of instability. Dig a snow pit as deep as you can (to the ground, or at least six feet); look for sliding surfaces within the snowpack—layers of dense or icy snow to which recent snow has not bonded. Perform a shovel test to see if the snow shears off at any layer, and assess how much force was required to dislodge a block of snow.

The more interested you are in backcountry skiing, the more you need to know about avalanches. This is especially true if you plan to venture to mountains in the western United States and elsewhere. Read books, take courses, and ask questions of people with experience in avalanche-hazard assessment. The Appalachian Mountain Club (AMC) offers a good introductory avalanche course in Pinkham Notch every winter. (See appendix B, Recommended Reading, for good books on the subject.)

SELF-RELIANCE

Being self-reliant in the mountains has long been a basic ethic of mountaineers. Having the ability to be self-reliant requires proficiency in first aid and mountaineering skills. Just as important as these skills is a mind-set when heading into the mountains that you will not count on being bailed out by someone else if an accident occurs. This mind-set should influence your choice of route, equipment, and skiing companions.

Self-reliance is important on a practical level. Rescues take a long time, especially in winter. If an injury is life threatening, time may be of the essence.

A problem has developed in recent years as people have come to assume that a rescue is just around the corner whenever they head to the hills. Many people have become lazy or careless about preventive safety measures. Being in the mountains without extra clothing, first-aid provisions, and repair equipment is inviting trouble. The odds favoring mishaps always seem to increase in direct proportion to poor preparation.

The increasing presence of cellular phones in the backcountry is perhaps the best example of how people are substituting high-tech gadgets for common sense. Here's a modest proposal for backcountry users: Instead of taking a cell phone, take a first-aid course. Or a mountaineering class. Or an avalanche seminar. Instead of the false security of thinking that you can call 911 from the mountains, take comfort in knowing that you probably don't need to call for help. You can make good decisions, prevent trouble, and take care of yourself. That's the time-tested ethic of mountaineering. And it's your best insurance for being safe and happy in the mountains.

First Aid

Prevention is the key to avoiding winter emergencies. Recognizing signs and being alert to the condition of members of your party are critical. Medical emergencies in winter are a different ballgame than in the summer. The extreme environment increases stress on both the victim and rescuer, and problems can progress from minor to life threatening in a frighteningly short time.

All backcountry skiers and snowboarders should obtain training in first aid (see appendix A). Accidents can easily happen in the mountains, and your ability to administer the appropriate first aid can be crucial.

Skiers should always travel with a first-aid kit. The contents of each kit may vary, but at a minimum they should include an assortment of bandages to control bleeding (including a combine dressing or sanitary napkin), materials to treat and care for blisters (Second Skin and Compeed are two of the best treatments), an emergency blanket, and a triangular bandage. I also like to carry two Ace bandages and a lightweight flexible splint called a SAM Splint (made by the Seaberg Company: 800-818-4726, www.samsplint.com). The SAM Splint makes it possible to immobilize an injured extremity quickly and get on your way—an asset when a frigid wind is nipping at you.

Hypothermia and frostbite are the two most common problems in winter. I have been amazed to witness the way that *frostbite and hypothermia can develop extremely fast!* In a sense, these are social diseases: they should not occur if every member of a party is carefully watching out for one another. These conditions are entirely preventable if the early signs are recognized.

HYPOTHERMIA

Hypothermia is a condition in which the temperature of the body core—the area around the vital organs—drops below its normal level of 98.6 degrees. You will need a hypothermia thermometer to measure subnormal temperatures definitively, but the basic signs and symptoms allow you to make a reasonable field diagnosis.

SIGNS

Signs of hypothermia in the early stages include intense shivering, lips and fingernails becoming cyanotic (blue), mental confusion, slurred speech, and clumsiness, especially with the hands. The victim may become apathetic, lag behind, and complain of being cold. This is called *mild hypothermia*, when the body core temperature (taken rectally) is above 90 degrees. Oral temperatures are generally 1 degree lower than rectal temperatures.

Severe hypothermia—when the body core temperature drops below 90 degrees—is life threatening. A telltale indicator of this stage is that shivering gradually stops. The victim becomes extremely uncoordinated, even unable to walk without help, and speech may be slurred. Severely hypothermic persons often become unusually careless about protecting themselves from the cold: They take off their hats, leave their parkas open, and forget their mittens (this common sign is called "paradoxical undressing"). Victims often deny that there is a problem. Left untreated, this condition can deteriorate until the person is unresponsive or even unconscious.

What is going on here? The body is simply losing heat at a faster rate than it can generate it. The body loses heat in four ways: through evaporation (e.g., breathing), conduction (sitting on the snow or wearing wet clothes), radiation (from exposed skin), and convection (windchill).

The body gains heat from digesting food, engaging in physical activity, being near external heat sources such as a fire or a warm body, and shunting blood from the extremities and the skin to the body core.

TREATMENT

The basic principles of treating mild hypothermia are as follows:

1. *Stop heat loss.* Remove the victim from the cold, wet environment if possible. If you are near a tent or shelter, use them. When far from shelter, one of the most important steps is to *remove wet clothes and replace them with dry clothing.* This includes removing layers of wet polypropylene clothing as well. Hypothermic people are generally unable to generate enough body heat to dry out their clothing, regardless of what "miracle fabrics" they are wearing. Add extra insulation over the dry layers. If you have no dry clothes, at least wrap the person in something windproof, such as a parka or tarp.

2. *Place the victim in a warm environment,* if possible. Putting the victim in a sleeping bag with one or two other people all stripped to the waist can be helpful. This is often unnecessary if other measures are taken.

3. *Give a conscious victim warm, sweet liquids and high-energy foods, such as trail mix.*

4. *Get moving.* Once your partner is stabilized, exercise will keep him or her warm. It's also the best way to "get out of the woods."

Treatment of severe hypothermia is a much more complicated affair. Most experts agree that a severely hypothermic patient should be rewarmed only in a hospital; even then, the prognosis is not great. If the victim has been hypothermic for a number of hours, metabolic changes have taken place and rewarming too quickly can cause greater harm. The best option is to *evacuate a severely hypothermic victim to a hospital with as little jostling as possible.* The victim should not be given warm liquids, since that can cause blood from the body core to rush to the extremities, further depressing the core temperature. The victim should be wrapped in a vapor-barrier cocoon consisting of a sleeping bag, a waterproof plastic or coated nylon bag, and a reflective emergency blanket. A severely hypothermic patient may appear dead, but may actually be existing in a "metabolic icebox" with barely detectable vital signs. Administering CPR is generally inadvisable; chest compressions can actually *cause* heart failure in a severely hypothermic patient. A hypothermic patient is not dead until he is warm and dead. Give victims the benefit of the doubt—get them to a hospital.

PREVENTION

Hypothermia is best avoided, not treated. Here are some ways to prevent it:

❋ Eat throughout the day when doing outdoor winter activities. Your body burns an enormous quantity of calories to stay warm in the winter. One lunch stop on the trail is inadequate. Have snack foods accessible, and eat often.

❋ Don't wear cotton. If someone in your party is wearing cotton clothing, be especially aware of how that person is faring. In my experience, that person will often become mildly hypothermic by late in the day.

❋ Stop evaporative heat loss by shedding layers of clothing *before* you begin sweating.

❋ "If your feet are cold, put on a hat." This old backpacker's axiom is a wise one. Up to 75 percent of the body's total heat production can be lost through the head and neck.

❋ Prevent conductive heat loss by putting on a wind shell *before* arriving at an exposed area such as a summit ridge.

❋ Be extra vigilant on warm, wet days. Skiing when it is 30 to 40 degrees and snowing is classic hypothermia weather. Bring spare dry clothes, and be on the alert.

❋ Check in with your partners. "How're ya doin'?" I annoyingly ask my ski partners throughout the day. Be specific: "Feeling tired? Cold?" Make them think about how they are feeling, and give them a chance to tell you. Then respond: take a rest, add or shed a clothing layer, eat.

❋ Drink lots of fluids.

The last point deserves special mention. Many people assume that dehydration is not a problem in the winter because you don't sweat as much as in summer. This is a serious mistake. The combination of perspiring and exhaling humidified air can dehydrate a skier rapidly. Dehydration is especially problematic for people who are overweight, since they tend to sweat more. A steady loss of body fluids makes a person more prone to frostbite and hypothermia.

Signs of mild dehydration include headache and brightly colored urine. Prevent this by ensuring that every member of the party has at least a liter of water that is accessible, and make sure people are drinking. Keep your water bottle insulated, or put it inside your parka so that it won't freeze; insulated hydration systems are useful if it's not too cold. Avoid alcoholic and caffeinated beverages. They act as a diuretic, causing further dehydration.

FROSTBITE

Frostbite occurs when body tissue freezes. It can affect any part of the body, but parts that protrude are particularly susceptible. The ears, nose, fingers, and toes must be closely monitored in cold weather.

Signs and Treatment

There are two main types of frostbite. *Superficial frostbite* is indicated by patches of gray or yellowish skin that may be hard or waxy to the touch, although underlying tissue is still soft. The affected area feels numb, tingly, or very cold.

The treatment for superficial frostbite is to *immediately rewarm the affected body part*. This can be done by placing it against warm skin, such as putting a superficially frostbitten foot in a partner's armpit or on his or her stomach, or just placing a warm hand over a numb nose or cheek. Do not rub the affected part, as this can cause deeper tissue damage.

Deep frostbite occurs when a body part—usually a hand or foot—is fully frozen, including both skin and underlying tissue. The affected part feels totally numb and wooden, and it is difficult for the victim to move it. Deep frostbite is indicated by pale, waxy skin over solid underlying tissue. The body part feels like a piece of chicken just removed from the freezer.

Field treatment for deep frostbite involves first preventing further injury. Keep the patient warm and make sure no other areas are exposed. Thawing can be done only under sterile conditions, and the affected area cannot be in any danger of refreezing or having to bear weight. Thawing out a frostbitten extremity is extremely painful. It is almost always preferable to ski or walk someone with deep frostbite out to a hospital, where comprehensive medical treatment is available. If you rewarm a deeply frostbitten foot in the field, the victim will have to be carried out.

A person with deep frostbite should be evacuated as soon as possible. The victim should be fed plenty of fluids to decrease susceptibility to further injury.

Prevention

Don't wait for problems to develop. If someone is complaining of numbness or tingling in the extremities, *stop and deal with it immediately*. Waiting "just until you get to the car" can lead to permanent damage.

Preventing frostbite should be a group effort. When skiing on very cold days, or high on a windy mountain ridge, partners should check each other continually for any white splotches on the face, ears, and nose. Other pointers to help prevent frostbite:

✳ Avoid tight boots. They are a prime cause of frostbitten toes. If your boots are snug, it is better to remove one layer of socks than to constrict circulation. Better yet, buy new boots that fit. If you have been frostbitten in the past or have poor circulation in your extremities, consider experimenting with some combination of double boots, insulated supergaiters, and vapor-barrier socks.

✳ Mittens are warmer than gloves, especially when used in combination with thin mitten liners. Bring spare hand gear.

✳ Have adequate wind protection. Snug up your hood on exposed summits. Balaclavas offer additional face protection. Don't venture to the summit on extremely cold, windy days.

✳ Constantly wiggle cold toes and fingers. Run around or do jumping jacks to increase circulation to the extremities. Keep moving.

✳ Avoid direct skin contact with bare metal or cooking fuel.

✳ If someone is frostbitten, they may also be hypothermic. Look for signs of both, and treat accordingly.

RESCUES

If someone is hurt, you must be equipped to stabilize the situation, attempt self-rescue, and as a last resort, go for help. When dealing with an accident, your first responsibility is to yourself and the other uninjured members of your party. You won't be much help if you get hurt falling down the same icy gully that your friend just caromed down. After ensuring that no one else is in danger and the victim's medical condition is stabilized (i.e., they are well packaged and reasonably warm), you must make a decision regarding evacuation. If the victim is able to get him- or herself to a trailhead without suffering further injury, that is always preferable to waiting around in the snow for a rescue party to arrive.

Time is critical in the winter. Do not waste an hour making an improvised litter if you do not think you can drag it out on your own. If you are alone with a helpless partner, you are usually better off seeking the proper equipment and enough people to perform the rescue efficiently and safely than exhausting yourself and becoming a second victim. If you go for help, be sure you know exactly where you left your partner; leave surveyor's tape or some type of marker along the way if you are not on a trail. Bring detailed information about the victim's condition and the nature of the injury. This will allow the rescuers to respond in the most appropriate way and know what

Climbing to the summit of Wright Peak, with Algonquin in the background.

first-aid equipment to bring. (See appendix D for emergency contact phone numbers.)

A cellular phone is not a substitute for a first-aid kit. Surviving in the mountains depends on good judgment calls, not phone calls. Cell phones frequently do not work in the mountains, especially in winter when their batteries are cold. Do not simply dial 911 and wait for help. It often takes hours to organize a rescue, during which time the condition of you and your partners is deteriorating. If you can possibly get yourself and your party out of the woods on your own power without endangering yourself, you will be much better off.

SECTION TWO

The Tours

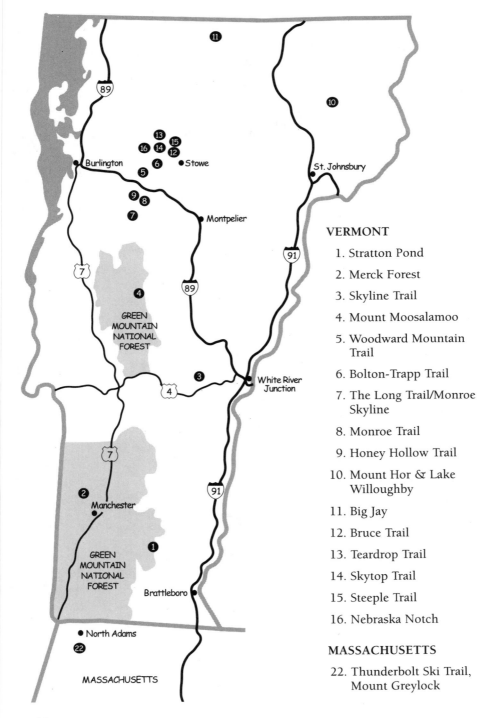

VERMONT

1. Stratton Pond
2. Merck Forest
3. Skyline Trail
4. Mount Moosalamoo
5. Woodward Mountain Trail
6. Bolton-Trapp Trail
7. The Long Trail/Monroe Skyline
8. Monroe Trail
9. Honey Hollow Trail
10. Mount Hor & Lake Willoughby
11. Big Jay
12. Bruce Trail
13. Teardrop Trail
14. Skytop Trail
15. Steeple Trail
16. Nebraska Notch

MASSACHUSETTS

22. Thunderbolt Ski Trail, Mount Greylock

VERMONT

A NOTE ON MAPS

The best hiking and skiing maps of Vermont are published by Map Adventures. The three maps that cover many of the Vermont tours in this book are *Northern Vermont Adventure Skiing*, *Northern Vermont Hiking Trails*, and *Vermont–New Hampshire Hiking*. These maps are available in stores in many ski towns, or contact Map Adventures: 802-253-7480, www.mapadventures.com.

Dates shown for USGS maps are of the latest revision of the map.

1

Stratton Pond

THE TOUR
A gentle ski tour on the Catamount Trail into the Green Mountain National Forest to the beautiful and tranquil Stratton Pond. There are several options for loops and overnight trips into the adjacent Lye Brook Wilderness.

LENGTH
9 miles round-trip (Kelley Stand Road–Stratton Pond)

ELEVATION
Start: 2,345 feet
Highest point: 2,700 feet
Vertical drop: 255 feet

MAPS
USGS Stratton Mountain (1986) shows the Stratton Pond Trail but not the Catamount Trail.

DIFFICULTY
Moderate

HOW TO GET THERE
From West Wardsboro, drive west on the Arlington-Stratton Road, continuing on the Arlington Road to the Kelley Stand Road. Pass the Grout Pond parking area and continue straight ahead. Plowing ends where the road crosses East Branch Brook, and there is a large parking area here. The Catamount Trail is 0.25 mile ahead on the snow-covered road.

ADDITIONAL INFORMATION
* ❋ Catamount Trail Association: 802-864-5794, www.catamounttrail.together.com
* ❋ Green Mountain Club: 802-244-7037, www.greenmountainclub.org
* ❋ Green Mountain National Forest, Manchester Ranger District: 802-362-2307, www.fs.fed.us/r9/gmfl

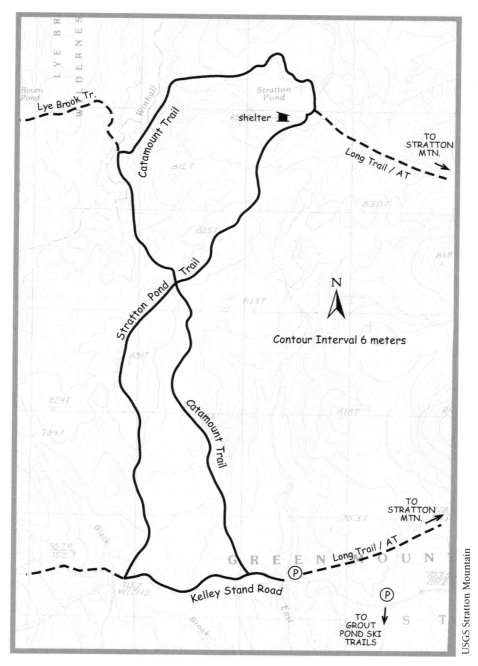

STRATTON POND

USGS Stratton Mountain

Stratton Pond lies in an unspoiled pocket of wild country at the southern end of the 350,000-acre Green Mountain National Forest. It is the largest body of water along the 270-mile Long Trail. The pond lies on the undeveloped west side of the bustling Stratton Mountain Ski Area. From the pond, you would never know there was anything besides trees and wildlife inhabiting the long, flat-topped mountain that dominates the skyline. Which is as it should be.

Stratton Mountain occupies a special place in the history of the eastern mountains. In 1909, James P. Taylor, a principal at Vermont Academy in Saxtons River, stood atop Stratton and peered out over the surrounding Vermont forests and mountains. It was here that he conceived of a long hiking trail that would run the length of the state. He helped organize the Green Mountain Club (GMC) in 1910, and by 1930, Taylor's dream—and the Long Trail—was a reality. It was also on the summit of Stratton Mountain that Benton MacKaye is said to have conceived of the Appalachian Trail (AT).

Stratton Pond receives the heaviest overnight use of any place on the Long Trail, with more than 2,000 campers visiting the pond between Memorial Day and Columbus Day. To meet the demand, the GMC built a beautiful two-story post-and-beam shelter in 1999 that sleeps twenty-four people (it replaces an earlier shelter that was removed in 1997). There is no charge for staying in the shelter in winter and no reservations are taken: it is first come, first served.

There are three routes in to Stratton Pond from the south. Hikers favor the Long Trail, which coincides with the Appalachian Trail here. This route, which is 7 miles to the pond, climbs up over Stratton Mountain. Hikers also can take a less strenuous route by heading in on the Stratton Pond Trail, which departs from the Kelley Stand Road 0.75 mile west of the Catamount Trail; it is 6 miles from your car to the pond via this route. Skiers have the best option: the Catamount Trail offers a quiet, scenic alternative route that is reserved solely for skiing. This is also the shortest route; it is 4.5 miles from the East Branch Brook parking area to the pond. Go light here: lighter-weight skis without metal edges will be fine for this moderate terrain, and climbing skins are not needed.

From East Branch Brook (which is also where the Long Trail/AT departs for Stratton Mountain), head uphill on the unplowed Kelley Stand Road for 0.25 mile. Where the road (a snowmobile trail) flattens out, the Catamount Trail departs north (right) onto a logging road. After 0.9 mile, the trail forks: the logging road bears right and the Catamount Trail heads to the left. Look for the blue Catamount Trail Association blazes to guide you at these junctions. The trail follows a logging road again, and after another mile crosses the Stratton Pond Trail. The Catamount Trail and Stratton Pond Trail form a figure eight around Stratton Pond, and this is the midpoint.

The best skiing is this next section. The Catamount Trail narrows into a woods trail and begins a delightful downhill cruise through a tall forest of evergreens. The trees tower overhead like totem poles lining the trail. Snow-laden

Ski skating across Stratton Pond.

branches occasionally deliver a cold slap as you drift through the forest. This is a woody, romantic place, and flying down through this intimate forest captures the carefree spirit of backcountry skiing at its best. After a long descent, the trail emerges from the confines of the forest onto the open frozen marshes of the Winhall River. The trail darts back and forth from forest to meadow, finally crossing a small footbridge over the Lye Brook Trail, which leads west into the Lye Brook Wilderness. The Catamount Trail continues straight ahead, then turns right and climbs uphill through the woods to reach the west shore of Stratton Pond.

Stratton Pond is a stunning white canvas amid a sea of green. Stratton Mountain appears as a long table top rising from the far end of the pond. It is hard to imagine in this quiet place that just over the top of the mountain is a veritable city in the woods—the "Upper North Side," as New Yorkers have been known to call it—complete with multilevel parking garages and packed lift lines. That realization only reinforces what a gem in the wilderness is Stratton Pond.

Spend some time exploring the pond. Follow a blue-blazed hiking trail as it bends around the north shore. If the ice is thick enough, you can ski on the pond itself. At the east end of Stratton Pond, the Long Trail/AT comes in. From here, you have the option of adding some variety by returning on the Stratton Pond Trail. While the Catamount Trail travels along woods roads for much of its way, the Stratton Pond Trail weaves a serpentine course through the forest. The trail is sparsely blazed, so route-finding can be a little tricky. You can make your decision on whether to ski it by checking to see if the trail has been broken out. If it has, the Stratton Pond Trail can be a fun, twisting ride back. If the trail has not been skied or snowshoed, it may not be worth the extra energy and time needed to break trail and route-find for another 4 miles.

Consider adding an overnight to your Stratton Pond trip and venturing into the pristine 15,680-acre Lye Brook Wilderness, the second largest wilderness area in the Green Mountain National Forest. Stratton Pond lies on the eastern boundary of the wilderness. In the early 1900s, the Lye Brook area was the site of a large logging camp and a railroad, which hauled timber out to Manchester. This once industrialized area has reverted back to a wild state. There are few trails in the Lye Brook Wilderness, so it will almost certainly be just you and the wildlife. From Stratton Pond, backtrack on the Catamount Trail to the Lye Brook Trail (sparsely blazed) which you can follow on rolling terrain to the South Bourn Pond Shelter. The shelter is next to the beautiful Bourn Pond. From Stratton Pond to South Bourn Pond Shelter is about 2 miles. You can return to your car at East Branch Brook by skiing south on the Bourn Pond Trail for 4 miles until you reach the Kelley Stand Road; it is a 1-mile ski east to the parking lot. A brochure and map of the Lye Brook Wilderness is available from the Green Mountain National Forest, Manchester Ranger District (details above).

Stratton Pond is a showcase tour for the Catamount Trail. This elegant passageway to a pristine mountain pond perfectly captures the spirit of backcountry skiing. It is a gentle ski path in the wilderness that serves up a scenic feast.

OTHER OPTIONS

The Grout Pond Recreation Area is one of the more popular areas for backcountry skiing in southern Vermont. Located on 1,600 acres of wildland, the area has more than 12 miles of trails that are exclusively for cross-country skiing and snowshoeing (i.e., no snowmobiles are allowed here). The terrain is generally flat, and views out over the pond are excellent. Trails here also offer access to the beautiful and vast Somerset Reservoir. There are seventeen campsites around Grout Pond, and a year-round cabin with a fireplace is available for overnight use.

Grout Pond is located off the Kelley Stand Road, about 1 mile east of the parking area for Stratton Pond. For more information and maps, contact the Manchester Ranger District of the Green Mountain National Forest.

2

Merck Forest

THE TOUR

A variety of ski tours through the historic and beautiful Merck Forest, with the option to stay overnight in cabins. A ski ascent of Mount Antone is a highlight, offering views over southern Vermont and the Adirondacks and a good ski descent.

LENGTH

5 miles round-trip (visitor center to Mount Antone summit); also numerous options for shorter tours

ELEVATION

Start: 1,800 feet (visitor center)
Highest point: 2,610 feet (Mount Antone summit)
Vertical drop: 810 feet

MAPS

* Merck Forest topographic trail map (available at visitor center and online on Merck Forest website)
* USGS Pawlet (1967) shows the terrain but not the trails

DIFFICULTY

Moderate

FEE

There is no fee for day use of the Merck Forest, which is open 365 days per year. There is a fee for staying overnight in the cabins.

HOW TO GET THERE

The Merck Forest and Farmland Center is located in Rupert, Vermont. From Manchester Center, take VT 30 north to Dorset. From the center of Dorset, continue for 2 miles, then turn left (west) on VT 315. The entrance to the Merck Forest appears on the left in 2.5 miles.

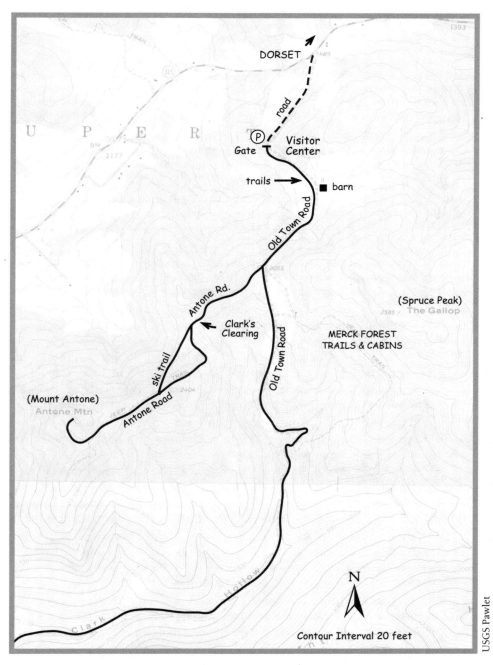

DORSET

road

P
Gate

Visitor
Center

trails →

■ barn

Old Town Road

2053

Antone Rd.

Clark's
Clearing

(Spruce Peak)
The Gallop

MERCK FOREST
TRAILS & CABINS

ski trail

Old Town Road

(Mount Antone)
Antone Mtn

2404

Antone Road

N

Contour Interval 20 feet

USGS Pawlet

MERCK FOREST

ADDITIONAL INFORMATION

Merck Forest and Farmland Center: 802-394-7836, www.merckforest.org

In the early twentieth century, the Vermont economy subsisted largely on the busy logging and agricultural industries. But what was good for business was not good for the land. Overcutting the forests and straining the capacity of farmland led George Merck to try to make a difference. The head of the Merck Pharmaceutical Company, Merck decided to purchase 2,600 acres from private owners in the late 1940s. He then set about trying to reverse a century of overexploitation of the land, beginning by reforesting his new property. He hoped to provide an example to others about proper stewardship of Vermont's wildlands.

Merck's legacy lives on today in the 3,150-acre preserve known as the Merck Forest and Farmland Center. Located in the heart of the Taconic Range in south-western Vermont, the preserve is committed to "providing educational and recreational experiences to enrich the lives of those who come here, helping them and others to become good stewards of the land." Founded in 1950, the Merck Forest is Vermont's oldest nonprofit conservation education organization. The organization has no affiliation with the multinational pharmaceutical giant that also bears Merck's name.

There are a variety of innovations at work around the Merck Forest. The entire operation is "off the grid," utilizing solar power for electricity. One building is made from straw bales, an energy-efficient and inexpensive building material. Animal-lovers will enjoy spotting wild turkey and seeing Randall lineback cows, a rare breed of cattle developed in Vermont that has a stripe down its spine. There is also an organic farm here, and a working sugarhouse which produces more than 300 gallons of maple syrup per year.

A unique attraction of the Merck Forest is the cabins where visitors can stay overnight. Each of the six cabins, which range in capacity from three to ten people, is outfitted with a wood stove and wooden bunks. An overnight stay here offers a way to immerse yourself completely in the beauty of this landscape.

A variety of ski tours are possible within the Merck Forest. The preserve is laced with 28 miles of hiking and cross-country skiing trails. The tours range from gentle slides down woods roads, to a ski trip to a working sugarhouse, to the ascent of Mount Antone with its dramatic summit views.

All the tours begin at the Joy Green Visitor Center, a charming post-and-beam structure named in memory of a longtime trustee. You may pick up a trail map at the visitor center, as well as other information on ecology and wildlife. From the visitor center, head straight out on Old Town Road. As its name implies, this path once served as the main thoroughfare to eight farms that were on the property. You soon come to the Hope Tree, a giant hollowed-out oak tree that you

Peering across to the Taconic Range from the summit of Mount Antone, Merck Forest.

can stand inside. The tree is a hit with kids. According to Merck Forest Executive Director Richard Thompson Tucker, the tree gets its name because "every year that the leaves come out, there's hope." Old Town Road soon reaches a large barn, where there are plans to have exhibits about local ecology and history. The century-old dirt road turns right here at a well-marked junction. The rounded summit off to the right (southwest) is Mount Antone (referred to as "Antone Mountain" on USGS maps but as Mount Antone by the Merck Forest).

Continue skiing along Old Town Road, which is wide and well graded. After 0.8 mile, Old Town Road reaches a junction with Antone Road, which is the route up the mountain of the same name. In the spring, Old Town Road may get badly rutted, since tractors use it to reach the sugarhouse. An alternative is to take the McCormick Trail, which departs from Old Town Road on the right, and then the Ski Trail. The latter ends at Antone Road. All of the roads, with the exception of Old Town Road, were cut in the 1950s by George Merck. He wanted to open up access to the forest for hikers and for fire safety.

Antone Road leads through a half-century-old stand of red pine. It is a pleasant, two-skier-wide path through the forest. The occasional ancient tree is sprinkled among the second-growth forest. The trail soon enters Clark's Clearing, a great raspberry patch in the summer which offers a broad view of Mount Antone. Just beyond the clearing, you reach a three-way trail junction and Clark's Clearing Cabin, a small structure that holds three people.

From this junction, the Birch Pond Trail heads left and soon diverges right to take a direct line to Ned's Place, a sunny two-story cabin that sleeps ten. The other two trails that depart from here offer a choice of routes up and down Mount Antone. The Ski Trail is a gradual climb up to the summit (skins are not needed) and is the preferred uphill route. The Ski Trail tends to have good snow conditions, since hikers and snowshoers are discouraged from using it. The other ascent route is to continue uphill on Antone Road. This is a steeper trail that receives most of the foot traffic up the mountain.

After climbing the Ski Trail, you rejoin Antone Road on the summit ridge. Views of the surrounding countryside start to open up here. Turn right (west) and continue the gradual climb up the mountain. Antone Road passes junctions with Wade Lot Road and Lookout Road, and finally reaches a four-way intersection just below the summit. The Masters Trail departs to the left (south). This is a steep, switchbacking descent which can be negotiated in good conditions by expert skiers. It ends on Old Town Road, from where it is a 4.3-mile ski back to the visitor center.

Antone Road turns right (north) and climbs a steep, rocky section for about 150 yards to reach the summit. There are two viewpoints: the actual summit and a larger clearing a few minutes farther up the trail.

From the summit of Mount Antone there is a classic southern Vermont vista of rolling hills and pastureland. A patchwork of farms covers the countryside below, while the long ridges of the Taconic Mountains march off into the distance. A description penned in 1867 by one Henry Sheldon, M.D., still resonates today: "The prospect from its summit presents westerly and northerly a beautiful panorama of forests and cultivated fields, mountains and valleys, villages, hamlets, rivers and ponds, well repaying the arduous labor of climbing its steep sides."

One striking feature that may be apparent from the Antone summit is the curious way the Merck Forest seems to attract snow. On one of my visits, I peered out from Mount Antone at a brown countryside, which miraculously turned to white at the boundary of the Merck Forest. Another note of interest is that there is a long-term plan to cut a ridgeline trail that would link the Merck Forest to Equinox Mountain, a prominent peak that overlooks Manchester. Such a route would make for a spectacular high-elevation tour.

When beginning your descent of Mount Antone, it may be best to walk the rocky first 150 yards back to the four-way trail junction. As you start skiing on Antone Road, it becomes apparent that skiers reap an unlikely bonus here: these old forest roads were meticulously graded and thus require only about 2 inches of snow to be skiable. Antone Road is a fast and fun descent on a 15-foot-wide trail. A good snowplow or short parallel turns on this moderately steep path will do the trick. For an easier descent, the Ski Trail takes a more gradual line back to Clark's Clearing.

The Mount Antone tour is but one of many ski tours you can undertake in the Merck Forest. There are numerous options for gentle ski touring on the valley floor between the cabins.

Richard Thompson Tucker muses, "The magic of this place is in the diversity of the experiences you can have here. For some, what's special is camping out and introducing kids to the outdoors. For others, it's being able to get into the backcountry and enjoy a day away from the hectic pace of our electronic lives." He notes that the forest is surrounded by protective ridges, and for people who stay overnight, "the stars and constellations seem to be brighter here than down below."

The Merck Forest offers a wonderful introduction to backcountry skiing. It can also be a great place to take kids skiing or hiking. The moderate terrain, beautiful vistas, historic byways, and overnight options combine to make this one of Vermont's most unique and prized backcountry getaways.

3

Skyline Trail

THE TOUR
The Skyline Trail travels a scenic ridge through rural central Vermont, crossing numerous farms and pasturelands.

LENGTH
6.3 miles

ELEVATION
Start: 1,600 feet
Highest point: 1,700 feet
Finish: 700 feet
Vertical drop: 1,000 feet

MAPS
USGS Woodstock North (1966) covers this terrain but does not show the Skyline Trail.

DIFFICULTY
Moderate

HOW TO GET THERE
From the town of Woodstock, take VT 12 north, bearing right after 0.7 mile and following the signs to the Suicide Six Ski Area. Leave one car at Suicide Six, turn right out of the parking lot and drive 0.25 mile to South Pomfret, where you turn left (north) on the County Road. Drive 5 miles to Hewitt's Corners and turn left at a road junction where there is a sign for Sharon. Go 0.2 mile, then turn left again on a dirt road. Go straight north-northwest on this road about 2 miles until it bends to the right and ascends a hill. Park at the top of the hill in the plowed parking pullout on the east side of the road (if you begin descending the hill, you have gone too far). There are blue trail markers and signs for Amity Pond Natural Area on the west side of the road which may be partly obscured by the snowbank. This is the start of the Skyline Trail.

ADDITIONAL INFORMATION
✳ Woodstock Ski Touring Center: 802-457-6674, www.woodstockinn.com

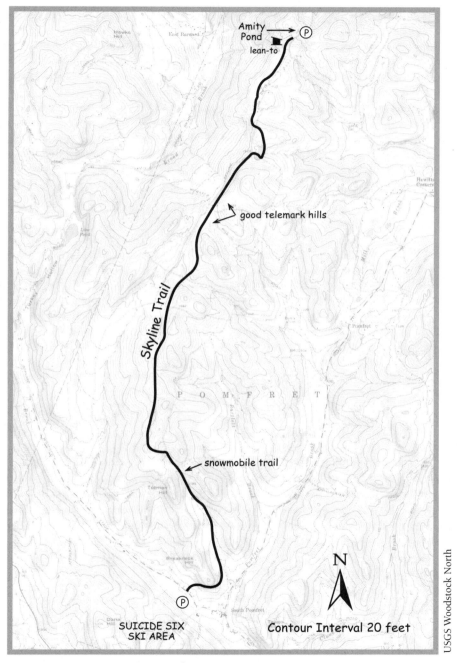

Amity Pond

P

lean-to

good telemark hills

Skyline Trail

P O M F R E T

snowmobile trail

N

P

SUICIDE SIX
SKI AREA

Contour Interval 20 feet

USGS Woodstock North

SKYLINE TRAIL

The Skyline Trail near Woodstock may do more to capture the spirit of New England than any other ski tour. It offers views that are quintessentially Vermont. The rolling pastures and farmhouses it skirts will bring a warm smile of familiarity to longtime New Englanders. Newcomers to the area will get a quick introduction to what it is about this part of the world that keeps people coming back throughout their lives.

This tour takes place in a historic ski valley. It was in Woodstock on the hilly farm pasture owned by Clinton Gilbert that the first ski tow in America began operation on January 28, 1934. The tow consisted of a Model T engine and 1,800 feet of rope, which cost a total of $500 to build. The rope tow was wildly popular, and within two years there were five such tows operating on slopes all around Woodstock and Barnard—one of which soon became the Suicide Six Ski Area. "It is said that farmers around Woodstock are obliged to sit with shot guns on clear winter nights to keep people from building tows in every back pasture," wrote A. W. Coleman in a 1936 issue of the AMC journal, *Appalachia*. A sign on VT 12 just north of Woodstock commemorates the site of the first tow.

The Skyline Trail exists thanks to the courtesy of more than twenty private landowners whose permission was secured. Credit for conceiving this trail and persuading these neighbors to allow access to their land goes to Richard Brett, a former resident of Woodstock who owned property in Barnard. Brett was eager to build a ski route that would connect his two homes. In the 1960s he began exploring where the route might go, and he asked local residents if he could blaze a trail through their land. He connected a series of logging roads, abandoned roads, and clearings in order to minimize the amount of new trail-cutting he would have to do. His original plan to connect Barnard with Woodstock never fully materialized. The northernmost section from Barnard to Amity Pond is a steep uphill climb that few skiers bother including, and the plan to cut a trail to Woodstock from the Suicide Six Ski Area, where the tour now ends, was abandoned.

The most popular section of the Skyline Trail proceeds downhill from the town of Barnard south for 6.3 miles to South Pomfret. A car shuttle must be done beforehand: drop one car at the Suicide Six Ski Area and head out in another car to the trailhead. This is where the fun starts. The trickiest navigation on this ski tour may be just finding the trailhead. If you've ever laughed at the frustrated attempts of a "flatlander" to navigate his or her way around rural New England, you may find that the joke is on you on this day. Just a few miles outside of touristy, bustling Woodstock, you are in the New England outback. Dirt roads dart off in every direction (except the one you are expecting), streets are never marked, locals have never heard of the place you are looking for, and you soon doubt whether you can, in fact, get from the proverbial "he-uh" to "they-uh."

There is a lean-to just in from the road at the trail's start at Amity Pond. Originally built by Brett, this shelter has since been rebuilt. A letter posted inside it expresses Brett's sentiments: "This campsite is a place to go to escape the din and cacophony of towns and cities, roads and highways. It has been a retreat from the trials of day-to-day endeavors and it has been a place to enjoy the intimacy of true companionship and nature." Camping is allowed in the lean-to on a first come, first served basis.

Just north of the lean-to is Amity Pond. According to local legend, the pond was so named because two girlhood friends from different nearby towns would come to meet and spend time there. Richard and Elizabeth Brett owned the land and donated it to the state, and it is now preserved as the Amity Pond Natural Area.

The Skyline Trail continues west past the lean-to, ascends a small hillside, and comes out into an open pasture. This wide clearing offers the first of many open views of the surrounding countryside. At the southeast corner of the field, bear left at a small white sign that says To South Pomfret (do not take the right fork to the Amity Pond Trail). The Skyline Trail parallels a country road, and blue blazes appear intermittently to reassure you that you are headed in the right direction.

The trail crosses a number of wide pastures and runs alongside stone and wooden fences that demarcate past and present property boundaries. The views and landscape are classic Vermont: rolling hills, the rounded peaks of the Green Mountains, isolated farmhouses, and befuddled-looking cows. This is not a wilderness trail in the pure sense, and that is part of its appeal. The signs of civilization, including the farmhouses and the unplowed roads, lend as much to the ambience and experience of this ski tour as open hardwood glades do to a remote mountainside.

The Skyline Trail meanders over pastures and into woods, passing through tunnel-like stands of red pine in the first few miles. The trail plays around, darting

Skiing across snowy pastures of central Vermont on the Skyline Trail.

up and dropping off an intermittent 1,700-foot ridge. After passing through a forest of birch and fir trees at about 1 mile, you emerge at a frozen pond with a large house straight ahead. You pass along the left side of the pond until arriving at a road, where you turn right and quickly come to a T-junction with Skyline Drive. Turn left here, and the trail enters the woods and runs parallel to the road for 0.7 mile, about 100 feet in from the road on the east (left) side. You may opt to bypass this short section of woods and just skate right on Skyline Drive if it is snow covered. Both the ski trail and Skyline Drive soon cross Webster Hill Road (plowed), and the Skyline Trail proceeds straight ahead (south) into the woods at an obvious blue blaze. Follow the occasional signs for South Pomfret. The ski trail coincides intermittently with a snowmobile trail in this section.

The Skyline Trail soon emerges at a farmhouse with an open pasture. This is the perfect place to stop and carve some gentle telemark turns. The trail then continues into the woods for 1.7 miles, and eventually passes a sign directing you to a scenic view. After crossing a driveway to a large house, you re-enter the woods and pick up an old jeep road. This is the start of a continuous 2-mile descent, during which the trail drops 700 feet. This final section of trail is also used by snowmobilers; be courteous about sharing the path. Note that this section can be very fast and challenging if conditions are icy. Skiers who are uncomfortable here can take off skis and walk, since the trail is almost always firmly packed.

The last 0.3 mile of the descent is a plowed driveway. You can ski it if it is sufficiently snow covered, otherwise you have to walk this section. At the bottom, just above a yellow clapboard house on the right and a red barn on the left, the Skyline Trail bears right through a gate and over a small wooden bridge. The trail rounds a knoll overlooking South Pomfret and the Teago General Store, then swoops down steeply (caution!) before ending opposite the Suicide Six Ski Area.

Other Options

Mount Tom (1,450 feet) overlooks the town of Woodstock and is now part of the Marsh-Billings-Rockefeller National Historical Park. It is crisscrossed by 30 km of trails maintained by the Woodstock Ski Touring Center. These trails are separate from the busy cross-country trail network located south of the historic Woodstock Inn (the closest Mount Tom trailhead is a 2-mile drive from the inn, and a more popular higher elevation trailhead is 5 miles away), so the area is lightly traveled. Skiing around on these groomed trails offers a fascinating tour of American conservation history, as well as an enjoyable ski. It was in this area that George Perkins Marsh, known as America's first conservationist, was born. You will ski through forests of larch, pine, and spruce that were planted in the 1880s by conservationist Frederick Billings and scientifically managed ever since. The skiing is relaxed, and there are panoramic views over the Ottauquechee Valley and a warming log cabin for picnics. You must purchase a trail pass and pick up a map from the Woodstock Ski Touring Center, located a half-mile south of the Woodstock Inn on VT 106.

4

Mount Moosalamoo

THE TOUR

A gentle woods tour up Mount Moosalamoo in the heart of the Green Mountain National Forest.

LENGTH

6 miles round-trip (from FR 32 to Mount Moosalamoo summit)

ELEVATION

Start: 1,600 feet (FR 32)
Highest point: 2,640 feet (Mount Moosalamoo summit)
Vertical drop: 1,040 feet

MAPS

* *Moosalamoo Outdoor Recreation Map*, available at the nearby Blueberry Hill Cross-Country Center
* *Vermont–New Hampshire Hiking* (Map Adventures)
* USGS East Middlebury (1983) shows the mountain but not the trails.

DIFFICULTY

Moderate

HOW TO GET THERE

From VT 125 just east of Ripton, follow signs for Blueberry Hill Inn, turning south on the Goshen-Ripton Road (FR 32). After 3.5 miles, see a prominent sign for Moosalamoo Campground. If there are no snowbanks and you can pull off far enough so you don't block the road, you can park here, taking care not to block the gate. Otherwise, there is a plowed parking lot 1.3 miles north at the Widow's Clearing trailhead. From Widow's Clearing, ski south on the Catamount Trail, which runs parallel to FR 32, until you reach a junction with the Horseshoe Trail (a cross-country ski trail from Blueberry Hill Ski Touring Center). Turn right and cross FR 32 to the Moosalamoo Campground gate.

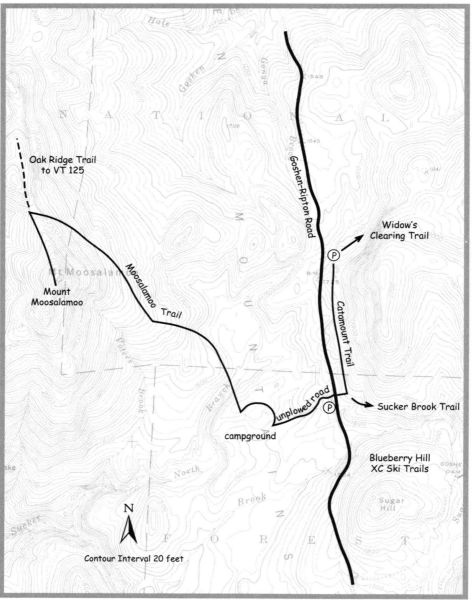

Oak Ridge Trail
to VT 125

Mount
Moosalamoo

Moosalamoo Trail

Goshen-Ripton Road

Widow's
Clearing Trail

P

Catamount Trail

unplowed road

P

Sucker Brook Trail

campground

Blueberry Hill
XC Ski Trails

Sugar
Hill

N

Contour Interval 20 feet

USGS East Middlebury

MOUNT MOOSALAMOO

ADDITIONAL INFORMATION

✳ Moosalamoo Region, www.moosalamoo.com

✳ Blueberry Hill Inn and Ski Touring Center: 802-247-6735,
www.blueberryhillinn.com

✳ Green Mountain National Forest, Rochester Ranger District: 802-767-4261,
www.fs.fed.us/r9/gmfl

> Two roads diverged in a wood, and I—
> I took the one less traveled by,
> And that has made all the difference.
> —"The Road Not Taken," by Robert Frost

The area of mountains and forest that lies east of Middlebury is a landscape that provided inspiration to the poet Robert Frost, who summered here for forty years. Visiting this area of lakes and wind-swept ridges, one quickly senses what moved Frost to such poetic heights.

The Moosalamoo region, as locals call it, comprises 20,000 acres within the Green Mountain National Forest. The area offers a remarkably diverse mix of terrain and recreational options. Both the Long Trail and the Catamount Trail traverse this area, which is bounded on the north by VT 125 and on the south by VT 73. Three different cross-country ski centers maintain more than 60 miles of groomed trails in this area, and the Middlebury College Snow Bowl is also located here. With its broad lakes, open meadows, and scenic mountain ridges, Moosalamoo has something to suit any winter traveler's tastes.

A variety of artifacts that have been found confirm that Abenaki Indians spent winters in this area before settlers arrived in the early 1700s. *Moosalamoo* is an Abenaki word that is thought to mean "the moose departs," or "he trails the moose." The area is home to black bear, moose, red-tailed hawk, owl, and the endangered peregrine falcon.

Lying in the heart of this region is the Blueberry Hill Inn and Ski Touring Center, run by the enthusiastic Tony Clark and Shari Brown. The inn has a deserved reputation for its gourmet Vermont food, and the excellent cross-country ski center has lured many people to discover the natural beauty of this area. Backcountry skiers are welcome to stop in at the touring center to get maps and information and purchase waxes and other necessities. Blueberry Hill is located 3 miles south of the Moosalamoo Campground on the Goshen-Ripton Road (FR 32).

Mount Moosalamoo is a pretty, wooded peak with views of the surrounding Green Mountains and lakes. The ski tour to the mountain begins at a metal gate across the unplowed road (FR 24) to the Moosalamoo Campground. Ski in for about a half-mile on this unplowed road until the road forks. There is a small parking lot on the right with a sign for the Moosalamoo Trail; it is 2.5 miles to the summit of Mount

Moosalamoo from here. Follow the Moosalamoo Trail, climbing gently through a scraggly second-growth forest. The trail has clearly visible blue blazes. The trail eventually comes out onto a logging road, where you turn right for a few hundred yards, then be alert for blazes directing you to turn sharply left into the woods. Descend to a wooden bridge across the North Branch of Voters Brook. You then commence climbing gradually on the well-blazed trail up the side of Mount Moosalamoo.

This is a delightful forest ramble. Make sure to notice the little things going on in the woods around you. Stop and try to identify animal tracks and notice where the deer wander (they often lead me back to a trail when I inadvertently drift). Take note of the winter sounds, such as the cracking of the trees as expanding water splits the wood.

Skiing through the forests up the flanks of Mount Moosalamoo.

At about 2,200 feet, the trail contours around to the north side of Mount Moosalamoo and continues its gradual climb. There are beautiful views of the frosted peaks of the Green Mountains across the valley. The Moosalamoo Trail suddenly pitches up more steeply and reaches a junction with the Oak Ridge Trail. From here, turn left (south) and it is 0.4 mile to the Mount Moosalamoo summit.

The trail along the summit ridge meanders around sheltered hollows. Keep your eyes open for the blazes, as the trail makes numerous direction changes up here. You finally emerge onto a wooded summit. For a better view, continue on the trail about 200 feet south of the actual summit, where there is a sweeping panorama of the Green Mountains.

The view from the top of Mount Moosalamoo captures the full diversity of the Moosalamoo region. Gentle knolls and meadows are punctuated by the sharp summit of Romance Mountain, the angular cliffs of Mount Horrid, and the sweep of the Long Trail ridge. To the west are glimpses of Lake Dunmore and Lake Champlain. Farther north, Vermont's Presidential Range—including Mounts Wilson, Roosevelt, Cleveland, Grant, and Lincoln—march off into the distance.

In determining your route back, it is tempting to try to ski a large loop, returning on either the Keewadin Trail or the Rattlesnake Cliff Trail. It seems like a nice idea when you look at the map—until you try to find these trails on the ground. When I skied it, the trails and blazes seemed to vanish south of the Mount Moosalamoo summit, and following the Keewadin Trail east was a game of now-you-see-it, now-you-don't. The surest bet, therefore, is simply to retrace your route down the Moosalamoo Trail. It is a pleasant downhill glide for much of the way home.

As you slide through the birches on the flanks of Mount Moosalamoo, you can imagine Robert Frost gazing over these hillsides. You will have new appreciation for the images that he conjures, like this famous passage from "Stopping by Woods on a Snowy Evening":

> The woods are lovely, dark and deep,
> But I have promises to keep,
> And miles to go before I sleep,
> And miles to go before I sleep.

OTHER OPTIONS

For an enjoyable, tamer taste of backcountry skiing, the Halfdan Kuhne Trail at the Blueberry Hill Ski Touring Center is the highest groomed cross-country trail in Vermont. The trail climbs the side of Romance Mountain for 2 miles, reaching a high point of 2,700 feet. From Romance Clearing, there are beautiful views of the Green Mountains and a long, fun descent ahead. This is a picturesque ski tour on a high-elevation trail where you can enjoy feeling "out there" without being too far out.

5

Woodward Mountain Trail

THE TOUR

A high-elevation ski tour from the top of the Bolton Valley Ski Area all the way down to the Waterbury Reservoir. The trail features excellent skiing and spectacular mountain views.

LENGTH

6 miles (from the top of Bolton Valley Ski Area)

ELEVATION

Start/highest point: 3,300 feet
Finish: 500 feet
Vertical drop: 2,800 feet

MAPS

USGS Bolton Mountain (1983) covers this terrain but does not show this trail.

DIFFICULTY

More difficult +

FEE

This trail begins at the top of the Bolton Valley Ski Area. A reduced-fee lift pass is available at the Bolton Valley Nordic Center for those who intend to ski only the Woodward Mountain Trail. Climbing up the Bolton Valley alpine ski trails is not permitted.

HOW TO GET THERE

You will need to spot a car where this tour ends. Take Exit 10 on I-89; turn briefly onto VT 100 south, then right onto US 2 west. In 1.4 miles, see signs for Little River Campground and turn right onto Little River Road. Go 1.8 miles and see a large parking lot on the left, which probably will be busy with snowmobilers. Leave one car here. Backtrack to US 2, turn right (west), and follow signs to the Bolton Valley Ski Area. At the ski area, purchase a reduced-fee lift ticket at the Bolton Valley Nordic Center, located in the Sports Center building.

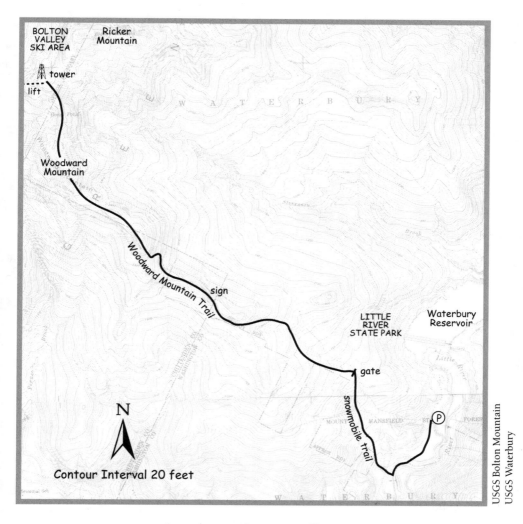

WOODWARD MOUNTAIN TRAIL

To reach the start of the trail at the Bolton Valley Ski Area, take the Mid-Mountain Chairlift (also known as Lift 2) to the Vista Chairlift (Lift 4). From the top of the Vista Chair, ski straight ahead toward a wood fire tower. The start of the trail (not presently signed) is a well-defined opening in the woods.

ADDITIONAL INFORMATION
❈ Bolton Valley Ski Resort: 802-434-3444, www.boltonvalleyvt.com

The Woodward Mountain Trail is one of the finest—and newest—backcountry ski routes in Vermont. It descends nearly 3,000 vertical feet over the course of 6 miles. The tour offers everything a skier could want: great views, powder bowls, fun skiing, glades, and long downhill cruising.

The Woodward Mountain Trail descends from Ricker Mountain to the Waterbury Reservoir. The route overlooks the historic Ricker Basin. From the 1790s to the early twentieth century, this basin was a thriving farm community with schools, homes, and cemeteries. In 1927, the nearby Winooski River had a catastrophic flood. The state responded by building a large earthen dam in Waterbury which flooded the old farm community. The abandoned towns are now part of Little River State Park, where the Woodward Mountain Trail ends.

The Woodward Mountain Trail was originally conceived of in the early 1970s at the same time as the Bolton-Trapp Trail. Gardiner Lane, the founder of the Bolton Valley Nordic Center, recalls that there was a grand plan for a network of backcountry ski trails that could be linked together and used for hut-to-hut skiing. The Bolton-Trapp Trail was cut in 1972. That same year Lane and some friends blazed the Woodward Mountain Trail, but they could not muster a large enough crew to cut the trail. So the blue blazes Lane had placed went unused. The Woodward Mountain Trail appeared on some old maps but existed mostly as a gleam in Lane's eye. In 1992, when Lane was seventy-eight years old, he and his friend Clem Holden—they dub themselves the Old Goats—decided to go hunting for buried treasure. They went hiking and rediscovered many of the old blazes, but they were unable to trace the trail all the way to the Waterbury Reservoir, and got lost twice while trying. So the Old Goats abandoned the idea once and for all. Or so they thought.

In 1994, Lane received a letter from some local backcountry skiers with a picture of an old trail sign that the younger skiers had discovered in the woods while bushwhacking up from Little River State Park. It was a sign that Lane had placed twenty years earlier. An excited Lane recounted, "Like the explorers Freemont and Lewis and Clark, the Old Goats and the Young Catamounts were stimulated and reactivated the work on the Woodward Mountain Trail." These "Young Catamounts" included Catamount Trail Association members Cilla Kimberly and Rich and Sheri Larsen. They promptly sought and obtained permission from the state to recut the trail, and a small army of saw-wielding skiers forged their way down Woodward Mountain in several passes between 1996 and 1997. Following a snowstorm in March 1997, the Old Goats and Young Catamounts together made the first descent of the Woodward Mountain Trail. Lane was eighty-three and Holden was seventy-three on the inaugural run. "The trail was steep, the snow was deep, the hearts were beating fast," wrote Lane of the adventure.

This backcountry tour begins, incongruously, on a chairlift. From the top of the appropriately named Vista Chair, ski straight ahead toward the prominent fire tower. The Woodward Mountain Trail starts as a discreet opening in the woods, but the path is obvious and clearly marked. Climbing the fire tower to take in the views is a required part of this tour—the panorama at the top is truly breathtaking. The full sweep of Lake Champlain, the largest inland body of water outside the Great Lakes, unfolds below you. There are views of the ski trails on Whiteface, Sugarbush, Mad River Glen, Pico Peak, Killington, Stowe, and Bolton Valley. Giant Mountain, with its prominent Eagle Slide, and Mount Marcy, New York's highest peak, cap the Adirondack skyline across the lake. Looking north, Mount Mansfield appears as a huge summit dome that has been blasted white. Bolton Mountain is the round, wooded summit just south of Mansfield. The nearby radio tower is located on Ricker Mountain. Look to the southeast to see the landscape of this ski tour: the long rolling wooded ridge line of Woodward Mountain, continuing all the way down to the Waterbury Reservoir.

From the fire tower, the Woodward Mountain Trail drops in an abrupt swoop to the southeast (toward the reservoir) then quickly turns right (southwest), passing just above the beautiful, isolated Goose Pond. The trail climbs gently but steadily up a ridge. This long wooded ridge running from northwest to southeast is Woodward Mountain. The mountain has four distinct peaks, all of which you ski over.

The Woodward Mountain Trail is clearly marked with red flagging and blue blazes. The trail snaps back and forth twice before arriving at a small clearing, where it proceeds to the east/southeast. The trail meanders through a high fir and spruce forest. Broken and twisted treetops are evidence of the powerful weather that pounds this high-elevation forest. This is a stunning ramble through numerous dark hollows that appear and vanish along the broad ridge. You are alone up here in a wild place. Bobcat and moose tracks crisscross the route.

A short downhill through a stand of white birch trees brings you to a large clearing at about 2,800 feet. Camel's Hump appears clearly across the valley to the south. After taking in the views, the trail begins to rock and roll. You begin a series of moderate downhills through the trees, where you can swing telemark turns or just ski straight if you prefer. Camel's Hump appears more continuously now, alternating with views into the wild and trailless Ricker Basin on the north side of Woodward Mountain. At about 2,700 feet the trail slabs around a

Carving telemark turns in fresh powder on the Woodward Mountain Trail.

prominent knoll that is one of the peaks of Woodward Mountain (the actual summit, which is unmarked, is 3,100 feet). As you descend, there are impressive views back up the trail.

The broad ridge is covered in open forest and offers numerous opportunities to link turns through the trees. You descend a number of small north-facing bowls. The temptation is to continue downward into Ricker Basin. Better to stop and yo-yo a particularly good section, as long as you climb out to rejoin the Woodward Mountain Trail. Keep your eyes peeled for double blazes, which signal abrupt direction changes. At about 2,400 feet the trail runs into a rocky outcropping on your left. The trail doubles back left up a short ramp to get over a small knoll. From here, there are views to the west of the Worcester Mountains and Elmore Mountain. Just beyond here, you come upon Gardiner Lane's old brown trail sign indicating that Little River Campground is 3 miles ahead and that Bryant Lodge, which is located within the Bolton Valley Ski Area, is 6 miles back. Ignore what the old sign says (the distances are incorrect) and where it points; the Woodward Mountain Trail makes a sharp right here and drops downhill.

The lower sections of the trail are south-facing and may be crusty. A long gradual descent brings you out to a clearing, where you bear right on a snowmobile trail. Watch out for water bars here in low snow. More than a mile of turns follow, finally bringing you to a large clearing and a major snowmobile thoroughfare. Turn right on the snowmobile trail and pass a yellow cabin on the right. Continue straight, descending the snowmobile trail. About 300 yards above the Little River Road, the snowmobile trail turns left and continues on mostly flat ground to the parking lot where you left a car.

A few words of caution are in order: There is no easy access on or off the Woodward Mountain Trail, and you are miles from help. Your party should be equipped to deal with any eventuality. Don't be fooled by the fact that the trail is only 6 miles. It crosses rugged terrain and you may be breaking trail. This is a full-day trip, and you should start early to ensure that you can finish in daylight.

Upon finishing the Woodward Mountain Trail, you will undoubtedly agree with Gardiner Lane, who reflected after completing the first descent: "Rejuvenation offsets exhaustion when you know you have skied an historic trail through many miles of beautiful wilderness without any mishaps."

6
Bolton–Trapp Trail

THE TOUR
A beautiful and exciting ski tour from the Bolton Valley Nordic Center that crosses over the high shoulder of Bolton Mountain and descends into the Nebraska Valley in Moscow. There is an option to continue on to the famous Trapp Family Lodge. This tour is one of the most popular sections of the Catamount Trail.

LENGTH
9 miles (Bolton Valley to Nebraska Valley Road); 11.8 miles (Bolton Valley to Trapp Family Lodge)

ELEVATION
Start: 2,000 feet (Bolton Valley Nordic Center)
Highest point: 3,300 feet
Finish: Nebraska Valley Road: 1,000 feet; Trapp Family Lodge: 1,350 feet
Vertical drop: 1,950–2,300 feet, depending on finish point

MAPS
❋ *Northern Vermont Adventure Skiing* (Map Adventures)
❋ USGS Bolton Mountain (1983) covers this terrain, but does not show the trail.

DIFFICULTY
More difficult +

FEE
You must purchase a cross-country ski trail ticket at the Bolton Valley Nordic Center to use its trail system to gain access to this route.

HOW TO GET THERE
If coming from the south, take Exit 10 on I-89; from the north, take Exit 11. Follow the signs on US 2 to the Bolton Valley Ski Area. The Bolton Valley Nordic Center is located in the Sports Center building.

To spot a car at the end of the tour, directions are as follows: From Exit 10 on I-89, take Route 100 north toward Stowe. After 7.5 miles, turn left onto Moscow

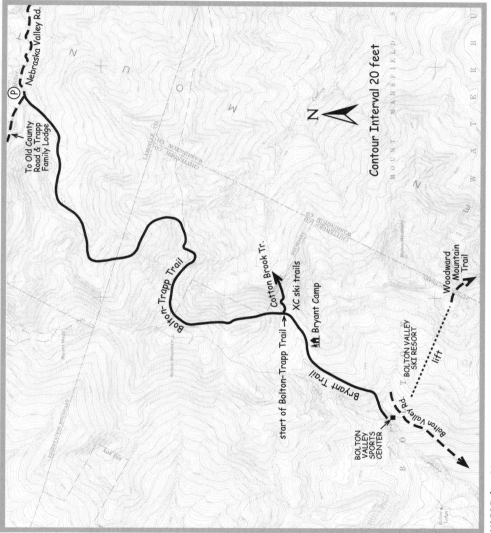

Contour Interval 20 feet

USGS Bolton Mountain

BOLTON–TRAPP TRAIL

Road. If you are spotting a car at the Trapp Family Lodge, turn right onto Barrows Road, pass the Stowe Junior/Senior High School, then turn left at a stop sign and follows signs to the lodge. If you are ending on the Nebraska Valley Road, pass Barrows Road and continue straight on Nebraska Valley Road for another 4.2 miles. Pass a plowed parking pullout on the left with a sign for the Mount Mansfield State Forest, and park in a second plowed pullout 0.1 mile beyond this. This is where the Bolton-Trapp Trail comes out. If this pullout is full, continue another 0.1 mile to a plowed parking area at the corner of Old County Road.

ADDITIONAL INFORMATION

* Bolton Valley Resort: 802-434-3444, www.boltonvalleyvt.com
* Trapp Family Lodge: 802-253-8511, www.trappfamilylodge.com
* Catamount Trail Association: 802-864-5794, www.catamounttrail.together.com

The ski route between the Bolton Valley Ski Area and the Trapp Family Lodge has become one of the most popular backcountry tours in Vermont. One reason for its renown is that it lies in the heart of Vermont ski country. The Green Mountains in this region are speckled with downhill ski areas, due largely to the abundance of snow that falls here and the quality of the mountain terrain. All of these attributes are showcased on the Bolton-Trapp Trail.

The Bolton-Trapp Trail traverses a remarkable breadth of terrain. Beginning at the groomed trails of the Bolton Valley Nordic Center, the trail travels through a wild high-mountain environment, descends a powdery basin, then offers the option of ending at one of America's most famous cross-country skiing centers.

An added bonus is the fact that this trail is part of the Catamount Trail, a 300-mile backcountry ski trail that runs the entire length of Vermont. Along its course, the Catamount Trail links more than a dozen cross-country ski centers (see appendix A for information on the Catamount Trail Association).

The one drawback of this tour is the time-consuming 30-mile car shuttle between Bolton and Stowe which must be done. One solution is to have friends who want to ski downhill at Stowe or cross-country ski at the Trapp Family Lodge drop you off in the morning at the Bolton Valley Ski Area. By the time their day of skiing is over, you should have arrived at the Trapp Family Lodge, where you can treat them to dessert in the Austrian Tea Room in exchange for their taxi services.

The idea of linking the Bolton and Trapp Family cross-country centers belonged to Johannes von Trapp, the founder of the Trapp Family Lodge. Von Trapp spoke with Gardiner Lane, the founder of the Bolton Valley Nordic Center, and they decided to undertake a joint effort to link their respective cross-country trail networks with an ambitious, over-the-mountain backcountry ski route. In the spring of 1972 the two men, each accompanied by a trail crew, flagged and cut their way up opposite sides of Bolton Mountain. They used old logging roads and abandoned trails wherever possible.

Von Trapp, who still runs the Trapp family businesses, describes himself as someone who "skis to get out into the woods more than for the sake of skiing." In the early 1970s, he imagined that the future of cross-country skiing would be ski touring in the backcountry, and that the Bolton-Trapp Trail would become a centerpiece of the Trapp Family ski trail network. He envisioned an ambitious European-style hut-to-hut trail system that would extend from Waterbury to Bolton to Stowe. It was a nice dream, but he was way off the mark. Skiers all but abandoned the backcountry trails until recent years, instead flocking to the groomed trails of cross-country centers.

The Bolton-Trapp Trail begins at the Bolton Valley Nordic Center, located in the Sports Center at the base of the Bolton Valley Ski Area. (Starting the route from the Stowe side would make most of the tour an uphill climb.) You must purchase a cross-country trail ticket before heading out, since you ski through the Bolton cross-country ski trail network to reach the Bolton-Trapp Trail. Don't be deterred if you don't see a lot of snow in the lowlands on your drive to Bolton. The high north-facing slopes on this route are renowned for accumulating and holding snow. The folks at Bolton Valley are a useful source of information on route conditions.

Leaving the Sports Center, ski out on the Picnic Trail, turn briefly onto Broadway, then pick up the Bryant Trail. The Bryant Trail rises gradually and offers views of the ski resort and the lift lines behind you, just in case you forgot why you were abandoning the crowds for the day.

You can stop at the small Bryant Camp hut for a break. It is the last outpost of civilization before the trail heads up into the hills. From Bryant Camp, continue uphill past the intersection with the North Slope Trail and turn left on Birch Loop. The trail rises gently, then forks: Birch Loop continues left and the Bolton-Trapp Trail heads off to the right. The blue plastic Catamount Trail blazes will reassure you that you are headed the right way. After about 100 feet, the Cotton Brook Trail leaves to the right; it drops over 6 miles to end at the Cotton Brook Road. The Bolton-Trapp Trail continues north, passing Raven's Wind (a Bolton Valley ski trail) on the left. The Bolton-Trapp Trail is clearly marked from here on with blue plastic Catamount Trail blazes.

The Bolton-Trapp Trail quickly switchbacks up into a grove of well-spaced birch trees with a panorama of the Green Mountains. Don't resist the temptation to telemark through this glade—God put the spaces between those trees for a good reason. The trail then climbs moderately, finally contouring along about 400 feet below the summit of Bolton Mountain (summit elevation: 3,725 feet). This area often has blowdown, evidence of the strong weather that hits this peak. After a series of short, steep climbs and drops, the trail swings around sharply to the east (right), where it follows the top of a ridge that separates the Cotton Brook Basin from the Nebraska Valley. The trail snakes through tightly spaced trees here and is often exposed to the full force of the elements. Don't miss the views of Camel's Hump and the Worcester Mountains at the end of the ridge. If you are getting buffeted by weather up here, you can take some comfort in knowing that the trail soon drops off sharply to the north into a protected valley.

From the end of the ridge, the Bolton-Trapp Trail begins a series of long descending switchbacks into the Michigan Valley. Skiing down is a delight in good conditions. The forest is fairly open, and the Michigan Valley is often a powder basin. Skiers can choose their route through the trees at will, dovetailing with the trail when it suits them. If you like what you find up high, you will enjoy the rest

Blasting through powder on the Bolton-Trapp Trail.

of the tour: there are 6 more miles of steady but moderate downhill on which to play.

The Bolton-Trapp Trail has a number of stream crossings, which may be open if there is light snow cover or if it is late in the season. After taking some final wide switchbacks through the forest and crossing a large stream, the trail parallels a brook for the remainder of the route to the Nebraska Valley Road. The trail drops down quickly and passes a small sugarhouse on the right. The trail soon enters a large clearing. This was the site of a farm in the 1930s and 1940s. The trail bears left here, following an abandoned town road that once served the farm. It is a sustained downhill from here to the trailhead.

Michigan Brook (unnamed on the map) is worth stopping to look at as you ski alongside it on the old town road. It constricts into a dramatic narrow gorge and has a waterfall near the old farm site, then continues as a boulder-choked stream down into the Nebraska Valley.

Once at Nebraska Valley Road, you have two choices. Most people spot a car here and end their tour. Or you may choose to continue into the network of trails of the Trapp Family Lodge. The final section to Trapp's can be difficult to follow; it is not unheard of for skiers to negotiate the backcountry traverse successfully, only to get lost in this little-used part of the Trapp trail system!

To continue to the Trapp Family Lodge, take off your skis, turn left, and walk up the road for 0.1 mile. A few strategically placed blue plastic blazes continue to mark the way. Turn right on Old County Road and walk 0.7 mile to the end. When you reach a house on the left and an open field across the street on the right, a trail (actually the continuation of the original Old County Road) leads straight ahead, with blue Catamount Trail blazes marking the beginning of it. This road-cum-trail has captured a stream, forcing you to cross from side to side. After 1 mile the trail ends on a large, open knoll where it intersects with the Russell Knoll Track of the Trapp trail system. From here, follow the Russell Knoll Track and Sugar Road about 1.75 miles to the parking lot at the Trapp Family Lodge Cross-Country Ski Center. Trapp's does not charge a fee for skiers who just use their trails to exit from this route.

This is a committing ski tour. The area between Bolton and Stowe is remote, which is one of the primary attractions of this route. The trail is not groomed or patrolled by either the Trapp Family Lodge or the Bolton Valley Nordic Center. Skiers on this route should be prepared to bail themselves out if problems arise. When the conditions in the north-facing Michigan Valley are icy, the trail is arduous and dangerous and probably not worth skiing. It is best to get information on trail conditions at the Bolton Valley Nordic Center before heading out.

The prize for skiers on this tour is the chance to traverse a wild region in the heart of ski country. This untamed "backyard" of the downhill ski areas is a gem.

7

The Long Trail/ Monroe Skyline

THE TOUR

Skiing the Monroe Skyline section of the Long Trail as it traverses the high, narrow ridge between Sugarbush and Mad River Glen ski areas near Waitsfield.

LENGTH

5.7 miles, Lincoln Peak (Sugarbush Ski Area) to Stark Mountain (Mad River Glen Ski Area)

ELEVATION

High point: 4,083 feet (Mount Ellen)

Low point: 1,600 feet (Mad River Glen and Sugarbush ski area base); 3,400 feet (low point on ridge is at junction of Jerusalem Trail and Long Trail)

Vertical drop: 2,483 feet

MAPS

* *Vermont–New Hampshire Hiking* (Map Adventures)
* USGS Mount Ellen (1971)

DIFFICULTY

More difficult +

HOW TO GET THERE

From Waitsfield, the Mad River Glen ski area is 5 miles west on VT 17. Sugarbush/Lincoln Peak is 6 miles south of Waitsfield on VT 100, then follow signs west on the Sugarbush Access Road.

The 270-mile Long Trail runs the length of Vermont, from Massachusetts to the Canadian border. Built between 1910 and 1930, the LT is the nation's oldest long-distance hiking trail. It is a rugged route through some of the most interesting

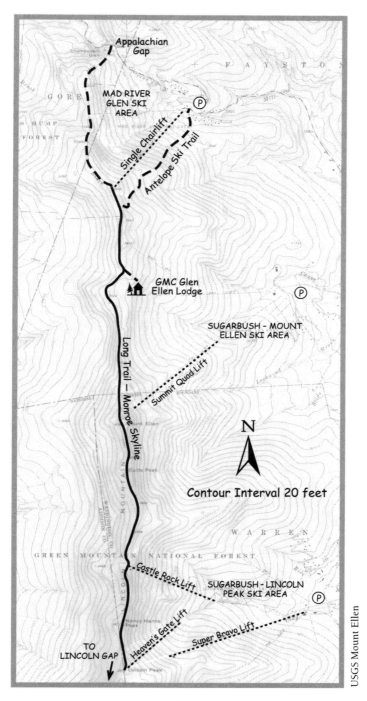

Appalachian Gap

MAD RIVER GLEN SKI AREA

Single Chairlift

Antelope Ski Trail

GMC Glen Ellen Lodge

SUGARBUSH – MOUNT ELLEN SKI AREA

Summit Quad Lift

Long Trail – Monroe Skyline

N

Contour Interval 20 feet

GREEN MOUNTAIN NATIONAL FOREST

Castle Rock Lift

SUGARBUSH – LINCOLN PEAK SKI AREA

Heaven's Gate Lift

Super Bravo Lift

TO LINCOLN GAP

USGS Mount Ellen

THE LONG TRAIL/MONROE SKYLINE

and scenic terrain in Vermont. The LT has 175 miles of side trails, and nearly 70 shelters for overnight use that are managed by the Green Mountain Club (GMC). The LT coincides with the Appalachian Trail for 100 miles; the AT diverges just north of Pico Peak (VT 4) and heads east to New Hampshire and its eventual terminus on Mount Katahdin in Maine.

The Long Trail is rightly known as Vermont's "footpath in the wilderness." Skiers take note: the LT *is* a footpath and was not cut with skiing in mind. In general, the LT does not ski well, since it is typically too rocky and narrow for most skiers' tastes and skills. Hence, the Catamount Trail, the excellent alternative created by Vermont skiers interested in long-distance travel in the Green Mountains.

Having said this, there is a section of the LT that deserves special consideration. The part of the Long Trail known as the Monroe Skyline runs from Middlebury Gap in Ripton all the way to the Winooski River in Jonesville. A lowland trail through this area was originally cut in 1913 by a state crew, and was designed both for fire control and hiking. But many GMC members were appalled that the trail never summitted any of the major peaks in the region. Professor Will S. Monroe took up the task of relocating the trail to the nearby ridgeline. In 1916, Monroe, a renowned botanist and psychology professor, began cutting a trail south from the the summit of Camel's Hump. A decade later, he and friends had completed a trail from Middlebury Gap all the way to Mount Mansfield. The high alpine section of the Long Trail from Lincoln Gap to Jonesville became known as the Monroe Skyline, in honor of the man who pioneered this scenic route. Historians Guy and Laura Waterman pay homage to him in in their book *Forest and Crag*: "Trail makers had found forest nooks before and climbed high ridges before, but Monroe may have been the first to combine such meticulous attention to detail with an overall skyline sweep. His work elevated the Long Trail from one that was merely long to one that was a classic for beauty and interest as well."

In 1925, Professor Monroe retired to what was known as the Couching Lion Farm on the east side of Camel's Hump. He died there in 1939, and is now buried, along with his beloved collies, at the foot of the mountain that he loved.

The Monroe Skyline between Lincoln Peak and Stark Mountain is among the most spectacular trails in the Northeast. Over the course of nearly 6 miles, the trail follows the crest of an exposed narrow ridge as it climbs and dips between 3,400 and 4,000 feet in elevation. The LT traverses the summit of two of Vermont's five 4,000-foot peaks in this section: Mount Ellen (4,083 feet, tied with Camel's Hump for third highest in the state), and Mount Abraham (4,006 feet), the southernmost peak of Lincoln Mountain. The *Burlington Free Press* effused about this section of the trail in 1919: "There were ledges one-half mile long and as the trail wound round these all sorts of fairy caverns came into view. It gave us a feeling that fairies, imps and gnomes scampered to cover just in time to hide from us."

The Monroe Skyline also links two of the east's finest ski areas—Sugarbush and Mad River Glen—and crowns the Mad River Valley, a historic and storied ski

Skiing the roof of Vermont on the Monroe Skyline of the Long Trail, with the Adirondaks in the distance.

community. This high and wild ski tour along the roof of Vermont has earned its place among the backcountry classics.

The Monroe Skyline trail has a checkered ski history. In 1919, a young Dartmouth Outing Club leader by the name of Sherman Adams took three friends and attempted a ski traverse from Middlebury Gap to Camel's Hump along the Monroe Skyline. They figured it would take them four days to ski the 43 miles. But the Monroe Skyline is not to be toyed with. The young men encountered 20-below temperatures and deep snow, and made very little progress. They soon bailed out off the ridge. Adam's misplaced cockiness on the LT was put to better use as an adult: he went on to become a congressman, governor of New Hampshire, and chief of staff for President Dwight Eisenhower. But as Adams conceded 62 years later to Guy and Laura Waterman, his abortive winter blitz of the Monroe Skyline was "obviously a foolhardy venture to begin with."

The Monroe Skyline continued to cast a potent spell over skiers. Ski pioneer Roland Palmedo, the founder of the Mad River Glen ski area, was enchanted with this ridge. After skiing the Monroe Skyline from Appalachian Gap to Lincoln Gap, he declared in the AMC journal *Appalachia* in December 1951, "Scenically, this portion of the Long Trail is unsurpassed. The ridge being as sharp as a church roof most of the way, one can frequently look down on the parallel valleys on either side . . . the area is one of the wildest and most unspoiled in the state."

Palmedo insisted that the Monroe Skyline "has the natural characteristics for a first-rate touring trail." In his article (written just after the opening of Mad River Glen), Palmedo proposed that the Monroe Skyline be maintained for ski touring by slightly widening parts of the trail, and by trimming upper branches that threatened passing skiers. His proposal does not appear to have been acted upon. But his intuition about the fine ski terrain here remains as true today as it was when he skied the ridge in 1950. In the 1960s, Palmedo spent time cutting and blazing his own ski routes on the north end of the ridge near Appalachian Gap. Skiers can still find his blazes, made from tin can lids, scattered around on trees in the area near Stark Mountain.

The Mad River valley has long been known by local skiers to be a snow pocket. The prominent north-south ridge that forms the western border of the valley benefits from "the lake effect": storms gather moisture over Lake Champlain and dump their bounty on the Monroe Skyline, Camel's Hump, and Mount Mansfield, the first mountain ridges east of the lake.

Two ski areas now divide up this landscape as follows: Mad River Glen is located on Stark Mountain (referred to as General Stark Mountain in the Green Mountain Club *Long Trail Guide*). Sugarbush consists of two main areas: Sugarbush/Lincoln Peak includes the ski trails on Lincoln Peak and Nancy Hanks Peak, and Sugarbush/Mount Ellen is located on Mount Ellen.

The best and most accessible ski tour on the Monroe Skyline is the section of ridge between the Mad River Glen and Sugarbush ski areas, a distance of 5.7 miles. The full trip from Lincoln Gap to Appalachian Gap (11.6 miles) is very demanding, and the gaps are steep notches reached by narrow trails that are extremely difficult to ski. If you do attempt a gap-to-gap trip, it is best done in two days, staying at one of the three GMC shelters on the route.

Which direction should you ski the ridge? There is generally an equal amount of uphill and downhill skiing whether you go north to south or vice versa. The more practical consideration has to do with the cost: Sugarbush does not sell single-ride lift tickets, so you must either ski up the mountain on the ski-resort trails (not recommended) or purchase a full-price lift ticket. Mad River Glen sells single-ride lift tickets and thus is a more affordable starting point.

To reach the ridge from the Mad River Glen Ski Area, take the single chair and exit to the left (south), heading down toward the Antelope ski trail. The entrance to the Long Trail will appear shortly on the right and is indicated by a sign.

If you aren't already familiar with the mystique of Mad River Glen, buying a lift ticket and taking part of a morning to explore the famous glades and "off-trail trails" of this mountain is well worth it. Mad River is much loved by a large community of skiers in the East who see it as one of the last "skier's mountains." So devoted are its skiers that they bought the mountain in the mid-1990s, making it one of the only cooperatively owned ski areas in the country. Mad River offers skiing as it used to be, and as it ought to be: there is no "out of bounds" here, no glitz, and minimal snow-making. You can pick your favorite line on this mountain and ski it to the bottom, regardless of whether it happens to be on the trail map. The tree skiing on the mountain includes some of the best powder runs around, and if you like moguls, Mad River is guaranteed to humble you. Mad River also has a large contingent of telemarkers, and is home to the annual eastern telemark festival held every March by the North American Telemark Organization (see appendix A).

Following is a description of skiing the trail from Sugarbush to Mad River Glen. If you are skiing it from Mad River, reverse these directions.

From Sugarbush/Lincoln Peak, take the Heaven's Gate Triple Chairlift (reached by taking the Super Bravo Quad, then skiing part of the Downspout Trail to Heaven's Gate) to the summit. At the top of the lift there is a small knob, which is the summit of Lincoln Peak. Sidestep up and take in the views; the entrance to the Long Trail is just off to the south. The entrance is obscure and there is no sign, but the opening is marked with the LT's trademark white painted blazes (which are fiendishly difficult to spot in winter). The LT can be very tricky to follow at the start, since nearby ski-area trails run parallel to it, and numerous tracks from skiers heading to their favorite off-piste powder stashes crisscross this area. Within a half-mile the ridge becomes narrow enough that all trails along its top merge.

The Long Trail wends through the woods until emerging at Nancy Hanks Peak, which is home to the top lift station of the Castlerock Chairlift. There is also a warming hut here. Castlerock is a Mad River-style expert area of natural-snow skiing within Sugarbush. Turn left at the lift station and follow the Middle Earth Trail until you spot a sign for the LT, where you head back into the woods. The trail climbs to Cutts Peak and then continues on easy ground to the summit of Mount Ellen, just beyond which you emerge again at the top station of a chairlift from Sugarbush/Mount Ellen. Bear left and ski along the left side of the Panorama trail. The LT departs from a small clearing on the left just as the ski trail bears right to join Exterminator.

Before pushing on, you should do a time and energy check here. It is 2.8 miles farther to Mad River Glen, and there are no bailout options in between the two ski areas. If your party is tired or it is later than you thought, consider heading down here on the Sugarbush ski trails. As airplane pilots say, "It's better to be down there wishing you were up here, than to be up here wishing you were down there."

The stretch of the Monroe Skyline from Sugarbush to Mad River Glen is isolated and beautiful. There are alternating views of the Adirondacks and Lake Champlain to the west and the Green Mountains to the east. This section involves some short, steep climbs and swooping drops. After 1.8 miles you reach the junction with the Jerusalem Trail (the lowest point on the ridge), and a little farther, a junction with a spur trail to Glen Ellen Lodge, a GMC shelter that was built in 1933. From here the trail climbs steeply, finally leveling off on the long summit ridge of Stark Mountain. The LT exits onto the Antelope ski trail of Mad River Glen. Turn right, and this beautiful, winding intermediate trail is the easiest way down the mountain. All the other trails from the summit are expert runs.

Skiing the Monroe Skyline is a committing undertaking. If you are not comfortable skiing down short sections through tight trees and making quick turns, this ski tour is probably not for you. There are also some mountaineering considerations to take into account. Weather can move in very fast, in which case you are in a poor position to seek shelter. Start early in the day: skiing this route will almost certainly take longer than you think, since the white trail blazes are often obliterated by snow and route-finding can be tricky (woe be to those who assume a ridgeline trail always goes straight!). Skiers should be comfortable navigating with a map and compass, and should be carrying both. The best advice for staying on route is to let the topography guide you. The trail generally follows the top of the ridge, although it wanders back and forth in places. If you begin descending off either side of the ridge, you are going the wrong way. This is also a fairly remote tour, and your party should be equipped to deal with any contingency.

One hazard deserves special mention on this route. With 5 to 10 feet or more of snow on this summer hiking trail, you are basically skiing through the tops of the trees. Spiky spruce and fir branches crowd the narrow trail and can easily catch you unaware, causing serious injury. The LT is not groomed to accommodate skiers, and for this reason *wearing eye protection is essential*.

A nice feature of this tour is that there are a number of places where you can bail out. The trails of Sugarbush/Mount Ellen or Castle Rock can be used for a quick exit if you are either moving more slowly than you'd planned or if there is a mishap. Sugarbush also runs a shuttle bus between its two mountains. If you haven't spotted a vehicle at both ends of the route, you can take the free shuttle from Sugarbush/Lincoln Peak to Mount Ellen and hitch a ride the rest of the way to Mad River to retrieve your car. Alternatively, there's always the time-honored tradition of going to the ski area bar and offering to buy a beer afterwards for anyone who will give you a lift all the way to your car.

These cautions heeded, this is a unique and beautiful ski tour in a spectacular setting. It is a dramatic introduction to this famous skier's valley.

CAMEL'S HUMP

No mountain is as beloved by Vermonters as Camel's Hump. The distinctive profile of this peak has come to symbolize the iconoclastic character of the state. Camel's Hump is indeed unique. It is the only undeveloped high peak in Vermont, meaning it is the only big mountain that you can ski all the way around without running into a chairlift. In a state that is home to dozens of destination ski resorts, that counts for a lot.

Many a developer has fantasized about Camel's Hump over the years. There have been proposals to build ski resorts and communications towers on the mountain. But the state of Vermont declared the summit a Natural Area in 1965, and extended protection to the rest of the mountain in 1969 by making it part of Camel's Hump Forest Reserve. The summit was designated a National Natural Landmark in 1968. The effort to preserve Camel's Hump began in 1911, when Colonel Joseph Battell of Middlebury, Vermont, made a gift of 1,000 acres, including the summit, to the state. Camel's Hump State Park is presently about 24,000 acres.

Camel's Hump is visible from downtown Burlington and from more than 20 miles away as you approach it from the southeast on I-89. Its three-tiered summit cone resembles the profile of a lion. But the debate over just what the summit resembles has raged for years. The Green Mountain Club *Long Trail Guide* recounts the story:

> The Waubanaukee Indians called Camel's Hump "the saddle mountain," and Samuel de Champlain's explorers named it *le lion couchant*, translated "the couching [not crouching] lion" or, in more contemporary language, "the sleeping lion." Either name is more descriptive of the mountain's profile seen from the east or west than is Camel's Hump, a name amended by Zadock Thompson in 1830 from the less genteel "Camel's Rump" listed on Ira Allen's 1798 map.

Camel's Hump has attracted a loyal following among local skiers. One reason will be obvious to any visitor: the mountain is blessed with an abundance of snow (an average of about 18 feet of snow falls here annually). The mountain is also fortunate to have relatively open forests, making it possible to leave the trails and weave through the glades. Another reason is simply the aesthetics: Camel's Hump is a strikingly beautiful landscape. It is just as pleasurable to stand on its flanks as it is to peer out from its rocky summit.

Following are two tours that capture distinctly different aspects of this mountain's personality.

8

Monroe Trail

THE TOUR

The Monroe Trail is one of the most popular routes up Camel's Hump. There is excellent skiing on the wide trail and in the open glades that flank it.

LENGTH

6.8 miles round-trip

ELEVATION

Start/Finish: 1,300 feet

Highest point: 4,083 feet

Vertical drop: 2,783 feet

MAPS

* *Northern Vermont Hiking Trails* (Map Adventures) is the best map of Camel's Hump.
* USGS Huntington (1980) and USGS Waterbury (1980) cover this terrain but do not show the current route of the Monroe Trail.

DIFFICULTY

Most difficult

SNOWBOARDING

The Monroe Trail on Camel's Hump offers more than 3 miles of downhill riding with plenty of room to make turns.

HOW TO GET THERE

From Exit 10 off Interstate 89, drive into Waterbury and turn on Winooski Street. Cross the bridge over the Winooski River and turn right on River Road. Turn left on Camel's Hump Road and drive to the end (be careful to avoid turning onto one of several side roads). Where the road plowing ends at the last house, see signs pointing left to a short spur road, which leads to the winter parking lot.

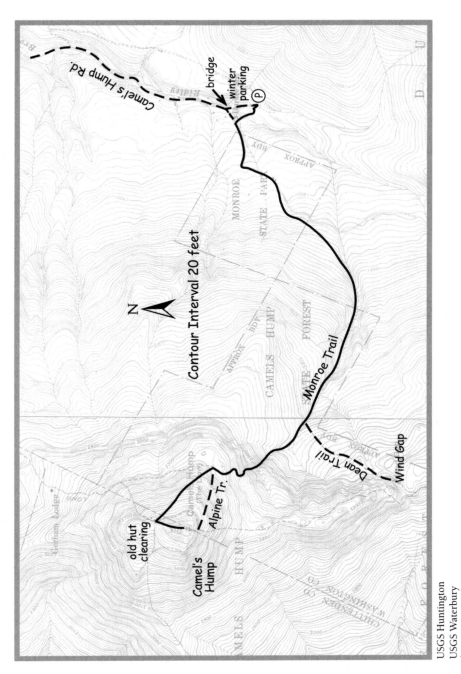

MONROE TRAIL

An ascent of Camel's Hump in winter is one of Vermont's most exhilarating mountaineering adventures. It hardly matters whether you choose skis, snowshoes, or a snowboard. The thrill lies in being able to travel through this remarkable landscape and take in its surroundings. The Monroe Trail is fairly wide and is the best of all the hiking trails on Camel's Hump for skiing and snowboarding. The climax of this tour is standing atop the wild, windswept, and icy summit of Vermont's third highest peak.

The Monroe Trail begins at the site of the old Couching Lion Farm. Professor Will S. Monroe, a botanist who planted a variety of trees on the mountain, left this farm to the state. His trees included white spruce, red and Scotch pine, Douglas fir, and Norway spruce, which were the source of wood for the caretaker cabin built in 1973. Professor Monroe, his sister Katherine, and his dogs are buried in a small cemetery just north of the unplowed summer parking lot.

From the winter parking lot, you ski through the woods to the snow-covered summer parking lot. The Monroe Trail passes a trail register and enters the woods. It begins on fairly flat terrain, then steepens moderately and maintains an even grade as it heads southwest alongside a brook. After 1.3 miles, you come to a junction with the Dean Trail, which departs to the left to go to Wind Gap and the GMC Montclair Glen Lodge. The Monroe Trail continues uphill until it reaches the base of some cliffs. The trail traverses left beneath the cliffs, crossing the Alpine Trail at 2.5 miles, then narrows and continues straight ahead, reaching the Long Trail (LT) at the former Camel's Hump hut clearing in 3.1 miles. This was the site of a hotel that went broke and then burned down in 1875.

Turning left on the LT, you can remove your skis at this clearing and leave them behind. The final 0.3 mile up the Long Trail to the summit is narrow, windy, and steep, and the summit cone of Camel's Hump is typically too icy and rocky to ski or snowboard. When you near treeline, it is time to don storm gear. The Camel's Hump summit is exposed to weather from all sides.

The views from the top of Camel's Hump are breathtaking. You can see nearly all of Lake Champlain and as far east as Mount Washington in New Hampshire and Giant Mountain in the Adirondacks. Mount Mansfield and the Worcester Mountains beckon to the north, and Killington Peak lies to the south. Most impressive is the vast sweep of wildland that surrounds Camel's Hump itself. The south end of the summit cone ends in a huge cliff. The summit is one of three peaks in the Green Mountains that are home to arctic alpine vegetation, which is typically found only close to the Arctic Circle. Take care when walking around the summit to step only on rocks and not on fragile vegetation.

Back at the hut clearing, it is time to retrieve your skis and descend. The initial pitch back to the Alpine Trail junction is narrow and fast. The trail opens up steadily below here, and you can swing turns down the trail. Or you can do as so many Camel's Hump devotees prefer: simply head into the glades that line the trail and make your own way down the mountain. This quest for the perfect glade run will keep you coming back to Camel's Hump time and again as you continue to mine its secret groves. It is a good idea to keep the Monroe Trail within site as you venture afield so that you don't get lost. Whichever way you choose to descend, you have 3 miles of gliding to thrill yourself with. It is the final reward for exploring Vermont's wildest peak.

9

Honey Hollow Trail

THE TOUR

The Honey Hollow Trail has a mix of fast downhill sections and flat skiing on gentle logging roads. It is a good introduction to the numerous skiing possibilities on Camel's Hump.

LENGTH

7 miles (Camel's Hump Skiers Association parking lot to River Road)

ELEVATION

Start: 1,300 feet

Highest point: 1,800 feet

Finish: 360 feet

Vertical drop: 1,440 feet

MAPS

* *Northern Vermont Hiking Trails* (Map Adventures)*
* USGS Huntington (1980)*
* Camel's Hump Skier's Association topographic trail map (available at the CHSA parking lot, or online)

These maps cover this terrain, but do not show the Honey Hollow Trail.

DIFFICULTY

More difficult

FEE

Skiers must buy a reduced-fee trail pass from the Camel's Hump Skier's Association to gain access to the Honey Hollow Trail through the CHSA network. Trail fees are paid on the honor system at the parking lot.

HOW TO GET THERE

The Camel's Hump Skier's Association is located in Huntington. From Exit 11 on Interstate 89, drive into Richmond, turn south on Huntington Road, and continue for 8 miles. In Huntington, turn onto East Street and go 1.5 miles, then

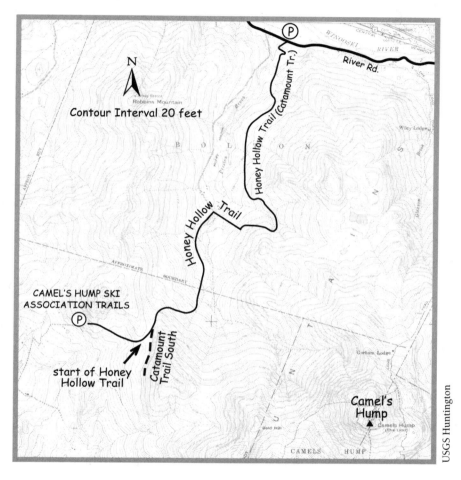

Honey Hollow Trail

continue up Bert White Road, and finally turn left on Handy Road. Drive 0.5 mile and park at the Camel's Hump Skier's Association parking lot on the left.

To spot a car at the finish: From Richmond, drive east on US 2 and turn right to drive across the metal bridge in Jonesville. Turn left onto River Road. A plowed parking area for the end of the Honey Hollow Trail is 2.2 miles on the right.

ADDITIONAL INFORMATION

✽ Camel's Hump Skier's Association: 802-434-4760, www.restinglion.com/chsa/welcome.html. Trail maps are available online.

✽ Catamount Trail Association: 802-864-5794, www.catamounttrail.together.com

The Honey Hollow Trail is a great sampler of the ski adventures that Camel's Hump has to offer. The trail, originally cut in 1980 by former Camel's Hump Nordic Ski Center owner Dave Brautigan and state forest rangers, drops nearly 1,500 feet in its 5-mile length. This tour has three distinct sections: a gentle 1.8-mile ski through the Camel's Hump Skier's Association trails, a fast 2.4-mile descent, and a rolling 2.8-mile ski on logging roads and woods trails. The Honey Hollow Trail is part of the 300-mile Catamount Trail system (see appendix A).

The fierce loyalty of Camel's Hump skiers is conveyed by the history of the Camel's Hump Skier's Association (CHSA). The association came into existence in 1996, when the Camel's Hump Nordic Ski Center closed. Local skiers were determined to preserve the cross-country ski trails that weave through the lower forests of Camel's Hump, so they decided to maintain and operate the ski trail system themselves. After obtaining permission from twenty-two local landowners to keep the trails open, the nonprofit skier's cooperative opened for business in the winter of 1996–97. Volunteers now groom and maintain more than 60 km of trails. The CHSA pays for its equipment through yearly memberships and trail fees, which you pay on the honor system in the parking lot. They offer a reduced-rate trail pass for skiers heading to the Honey Hollow Trail. This cooperative has been a unique Vermont solution which has maintained access to a cherished mountain.

From the CHSA parking lot (where trail maps are available), cross Handy Road and follow the access trail as it heads up into a large field. Ski next to an obvious line of pine trees that goes straight uphill. At the top of the field, join Saddle Road, then immediately turn right on Jack's Jog. Then turn left onto Pond Road, go 25 yards, and turn right on Woodchuck Ramble. At a Y junction, bear left onto Loggers Loop. This climbs steadily to the start of the Honey Hollow Trail, which is well marked. At the top of the last rise, you have a clear view of the profile of Camel's Hump.

Powder day on Camel's Hump: in deep on the Honey Hollow Trail.

The Honey Hollow Trail, which is well marked with blue plastic Catamount Trail blazes, begins with some long, straight, and narrow downhill chutes, followed by short, steep drops. These are a thrill in powder. The downhills are punctuated by flatter traverses. The trail then emerges onto a woods road, where you turn left and follow it downhill. At the bottom of a long downhill, turn right and pass through a gate, then climb on a "multi-use road" (blazed orange) until the Catamount Trail departs into the woods on the left. Follow the woods trail for 1.6 miles until it merges with a logging road, which leads down to the Honey Hollow parking area.

10

Mount Hor and Lake Willoughby

THE TOUR

A breathtakingly scenic ski tour on Mount Hor, offering moderate skiing and excellent views of Lake Willoughby and the towering ice cliffs on Mount Pisgah.

LENGTH

4 miles round-trip

ELEVATION

Start/finish: 1,300 feet
Highest point: 2,654 feet (Mount Hor, South Summit)
Vertical drop: 1,354 feet

MAPS

* *Northern Vermont Hiking Trails* (Map Adventures)
* USGS Sutton (1986)

DIFFICULTY

Moderate

HOW TO GET THERE

From the south end of Lake Willoughby on VT 5A, drive south 0.6 mile to a large plowed parking area on the west side of the road. This is the South Pisgah parking lot, and the CCC Road leaves from here.

Lake Willoughby, dubbed the "Lucerne of America," forms the centerpiece of what is arguably the most beautiful landscape in Vermont. The analogy to Switzerland's famous Lake Lucerne, which is ringed by the Alps, is apt. The fiord-like appearance of Lake Willoughby is created by the steep granite slabs of Mount

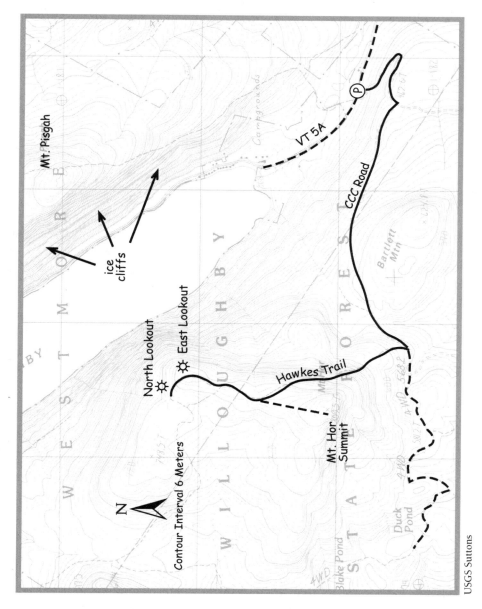

MOUNT HOR AND LAKE WILLOUGHBY

Pisgah to the east and Mount Hor to the west. The mountains rise precipitously from the water and appear like an open jaw (known as Willoughby Notch) swallowing up the southern end of the lake. The area has been designated a National Natural Landmark and a Vermont Natural Area, and is included in the Vermont Fragile Area Registry.

Willoughby Notch was formed about 2 million years ago when 10,000 feet of ice covered northern New England. As the ice sheet ground its way south to the ocean, it tended to ride up the north side of mountains and calve off the south side. This phenomenon is evident on Mount Hor and on nearby Wheeler and Haystack mountains. Willoughby Notch formed when a finger of the huge glacier reamed out an area of softer rock between Mounts Hor and Pisgah. Some of the glacial till formed the height-of-land at the south end of the lake. The final advance of the glacier pushed the rocks that were New England's mountains all the way to Long Island in New York.

Lake Willoughby and its surrounding peaks are steeped in colorful history. According to *Willoughby Lake: Legends and Legacies,* by Harriet F. Fisher, the lake is most likely named for the Willoughby brothers, lumbermen who held first title to lake-front property. The surrounding mountains draw their name from the Bible. As Fisher notes, "Mount Pisgah is the place where the Lord sent Moses to view the Promised Land….Aaron died at Mount Hor after the Lord commanded him to go there."

The lake-front road (now VT 5A) was built by a local tavern owner around 1850. He went broke putting in the road, but it may have helped bring people to his pub. In the 1870s, a forty-passenger steamship began operation on the lake. The boat sailed until the early 1900s. A young Robert Frost was so unknown when he visited Lake Willoughby in 1909 that he and his family were relegated to tenting on the site of the current Willough Vale Inn, now a beautiful restored structure with a hillside overlook of the majestic landscape.

Legends abound about Lake Willoughby's mountains. There is a well-hidden cave on the cliffs of Mount Hor, about 300 feet up from shore. In the 1930s during Prohibition, Fisher recounts, "some enterprising thirsty Vermonters used this cave to hide a whiskey still." The moonshiners concealed their activities by firing up only on foggy nights. But the "revenuers" apparently found out about the illegal activity. Hoping to catch the moonshiners red-handed, they raided the whiskey cave. The locals had been tipped off, however, and all the agents found was the contraband. The revenuers promptly dumped the hooch and mash into the lake. Locals insist that "the fish were drunk for a week."

The ski tour up Mount Hor is like skiing through nature's art gallery. Each viewpoint is more impressive than the previous one. Mount Hor features 1,000-foot cliffs that plunge directly into Lake Willoughby. This precipitous drop-off to the east makes the mountain a particularly dramatic perch from which to view the surrounding scenery.

Taking in the views of Lake Willoughby and the ice cliffs on Mount Pisgah (right) on the Mount Hor ski tour.

Starting from the South Pisgah parking lot, ski up the wide CCC Road, which is also used by snowmobilers. The Civilian Conservation Corps built the road during the 1930s. Climb south for about 200 feet and bear right at a junction, heading back toward the lake. Ski due west, soon coming to a broad viewpoint of Mount Pisgah and the lake. Continue west, bearing right at another junction and eventually coming to a prominent sign for Willoughby State Forest. This state forest, established in 1928, covers 7,300 acres and encompasses both Mount Hor and Mount Pisgah. You continue your approach on the CCC Road for 1.7 miles, where you reach a trailhead sign for the Herbert Hawkes Trail.

The Herbert Hawkes Trail rises for 0.7 mile, following a woods road to the trail junction on the Mount Hor summit ridge. Passing the sign, you ascend an unblazed but obvious old woods path. A few minutes after you start, bear right toward Mount Pisgah, avoiding another old logging road that appears to drift off to the left. Meander gradually up through the forest on the wide path until you arrive on a ridge where there is a view of the lake. The woods road peters out here, and the trail makes a sharp left turn up a small drainage. There are some intermittent navy blue blazes, but they appear to start and stop arbitrarily. The trail steepens a bit until finally arriving at a junction with the North Trail. From here, turn left and go 0.3 mile to the South Summit of Mount Hor, the highest point on the mountain. There are limited views from this wooded summit. The better option is to turn right (north), and head 0.6 mile to East Lookout and 0.7 mile to North Lookout.

The North Trail contours along the west side of the summit ridge, with intermittent views of Mount Pisgah and the ice cliffs to the east. The trail is faintly marked with light blue blazes. Even if you temporarily lose the blazes, you will do fine if you just continue to contour along the top of the relatively flat ridge. After some pleasant kicking and gliding along, you arrive at an old sign for the East Lookout. The lookout is about 100 feet farther downhill, but you would be wise to remove skis here and walk down to the viewpoint—it is the top of a cliff!

From the East Lookout, there are expansive views all the way to Burke Mountain. But the main attraction is what stares at you from across the lake: the ice cliffs that pour over the west face of Mount Pisgah. If you look closely, you will probably see ice climbers crabbing their way skyward. Willoughby, as this climbing area is known, boasts some of the most technically challenging ice climbing routes in the East. This enormous wall of blue ice extends for about 1 mile. Beyond it are the rolling hills of the Northeast Kingdom. Looking straight down, you are peering into the jaws of Willoughby Notch, which you now stand atop.

Continuing north on the trail for another 0.1 mile, you descend a short way to reach the North Lookout (no sign). From here, a panorama unfolds of the entire northern end of Lake Willoughby. You can survey the busy activities of the winter communities of ice fishermen that spring up on the lake. This transitory shantytown has the life span of the sheet of ice that covers the lake. As the ice vaporizes, so too does this community.

The skiing along the ridge is fast and fun, with little perceptible gain or loss in elevation. The best downhill skiing lies just below the junction with the Herbert Hawkes Trail. The trail follows a sidehill at the start until turning left and descending through open hardwoods. You can drop into woods virtually anywhere you like and you will be assured of crossing your tracks from the ascent. The trail out is wide and gentle, a fun couple miles of cruising back to your car.

Other Options

Mount Pisgah (2,752 feet) is a more challenging ski than Mount Hor. It is 1.7 miles from VT 5A to the summit of Mount Pisgah via the South Trail. It offers great views of Mount Hor and Lake Willoughby.

The **CCC Road** is a relaxed and popular cross-country ski tour. Beyond the Henry Hawkes trailhead, continue straight on the CCC Road, bearing right at two junctions. The trail eventually reaches Duck, Blake, and Vail ponds. These beautiful frozen waterways are excellent places to spot wildlife.

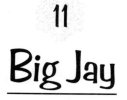

11

Big Jay

THE TOUR
A descent of the steep, trailless East Face of Big Jay, one of the best backcountry powder runs in the Northeast.

LENGTH
3.5 miles (Jay Peak–Big Jay Summit–VT 242)

ELEVATION
Highest points: 3,861 (Jay Peak); 3,786 feet (Big Jay)
Finish: 1,650 feet
Vertical drop: 2,136 feet

MAPS
USGS Jay Peak (1986)

DIFFICULTY
Most difficult

FEE
You must purchase a Jay Peak Ski Area lift ticket to take the tramway to the summit of Jay Peak. Single-ride tram tickets are available.

SNOWBOARDING
Big Jay is a popular backcountry snowboard descent. Its steep pitch and fairly continuous drop make it a great snowboard tour. You will need snowshoes for the climb.

HOW TO GET THERE
Take VT 242 to Jay Peak Resort, where you can park. Purchase a lift ticket and ride the aerial tramway to the summit. Directions to Big Jay follow.

ADDITIONAL INFORMATION
  ❄ Jay Peak Resort: 802-988-2611, www.jaypeakresort.com
  ❄ Green Mountain Club: 802-244-7037, www.greenmountainclub.org

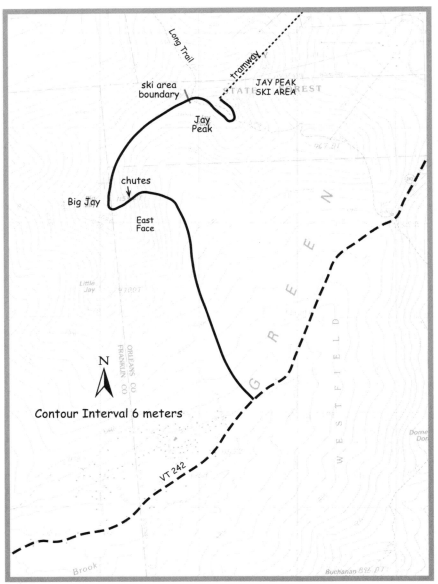

Contour Interval 6 meters

USGS Jay Peak

Big Jay

Hikers and skiers have long peered out from the summit of Jay Peak into the wild and seemingly inaccessible reaches of the surrounding mountains. There are views from the rocky summit out over the Cold Hollow Mountains, a trailless mountain range to the south, and as far away as Mount Mansfield and the Adirondacks.

One nearby mountain is particularly alluring. As you step off the Jay Peak aerial tramway, you peer directly at the improbably steep flanks of Big Jay, the trailless peak to the southwest. The sister peaks are joined by a long ridge that curves around to form a horseshoe. A large trackless basin is formed between the two mountains. It is in this basin that skiers have for years been poking around in search of powder shots. The most captivating prospect is a prominent white chute that splits the East Face of Big Jay.

For many years, the few intrepid skiers who ventured out to Big Jay would describe to disbelieving friends the powdery riches they had to themselves. But throughout the 1990s, as skiers and snowboarders have pushed their quest for adventure and powder farther into untamed lands, word about the powder fields hidden on the East Face of Big Jay has spread through the grapevine like fire in dry grass. If "steep and deep" defines your winter passion, Big Jay will not disappoint.

The Jay Peak Ski Area has long boasted of having the greatest natural snowfall in the East. While locals view the hyperbolic Jay Peak snow reports with skepticism, it is fair to say that Jay Peak is typically better endowed with snow than mountains to its south. It is also less traveled than the big resorts in central and southern Vermont. That translates into fairly reliable fresh tracks for powderhounds who make the trip to this outpost on the Canadian border.

Big Jay is the second highest peak in the Green Mountains without a maintained trail (Mendon Peak, near Killington is the highest). It is home to a variety of plant and wildlife habitats, including the endangered peregrine falcon, Canada lynx, and Bicknell's thrush, which live on the summit. The mountain was included as part of a 1,573-acre parcel that was purchased in 1993 by the Green Mountain Club, with the help of the Vermont Housing and Conservation Board, for the Long Trail Protection Campaign. This parcel, which is now part of the Jay State Forest, also includes 1.3 miles of the Long Trail. The Green Mountain Club and the Vermont Housing and Conservation Board hold a conservation easement on the peak, ensuring that the mountain will remain undeveloped.

For years, the occasional skier from neighboring Jay Peak left the ski area and endured a two-hour-long bushwhack up to the summit of Big Jay. It was not an easy jaunt, but it was all part of "earning your turns." Throughout the 1990s, Jay Peak Ski Area, like many ski resorts, became increasingly interested in promoting adventure skiing and snowboarding. The ski area eventually began leading guided tours out to Big Jay, and in 1998 a Jay Peak Ski Area trail crew cut an illegal trail all the way out to the summit of this wild mountain. The Green Mountain Club cried foul, charging that this was a blatant violation both of its conservation easement and of Big Jay's designation as a trailless peak. Jay Peak apologized, promised to contribute toward a GMC endowment fund, and pledged to remediate the damage.

This explains why there has come to be a trail to the summit of this trailless peak. Backcountry skiers and riders may view this unfortunate development with guilty pleasure: the result is that it is now considerably easier and faster to reach the summit of one of Vermont's best powder stashes. However, please note that *there should be no further trail cutting on Big Jay*. The natural corridors provide plenty of room for skiers and riders, and the special character of this mountain derives from its remoteness and its unimproved state.

From the Jay Peak aerial tramway, descend on the Northway. Follow the ski trail around a U-turn, continue for another 100 yards, and arrive at a clearly marked ski area boundary. Signs warn that you are leaving the ski area, and if you ski beyond this point, you will be billed for rescue if one is needed. Suffice it to say that you have been warned. Just because you are starting at a ski area, do not treat this as a casual resort run. This is a bona fide backcountry tour, and you should be carrying the appropriate clothing, food, equipment, and repair gear that you will need to be self-sufficient in case anything goes wrong.

The trail up Big Jay begins beyond the ski area boundary signs. It is 1 mile from the ski area boundary to the Big Jay summit. The trail stays atop a well-defined ridge, descends for about 220 feet, then climbs for 400 feet to gain the summit. The trail generally follows the south side of the ridge, affording good views into the bowl between Jay Peak and Big Jay. Avoid the temptation to veer to the north side of the ridge; it will not lead to the summit, and may lure you into the inaccessible Black Falls Basin, which is many hours from the road. On the final steep section of the climb, there are spectacular views that extend from Mount Washington in New Hampshire to Mount Marcy in New York. You are overlooking some of the wildest stretches of the Vermont mountains up here. That is one of the appeals of this tour.

The summit of Big Jay is a somewhat nondescript wooded plateau. To break out onto the East Face where the good skiing and riding are, continue straight ahead (south) on the ridge for about 150 feet. Then turn left onto the face, negotiating tight trees at the top. There is no formal trail or entrance, and the route onto the face is indistinct at first. But bear to the left as you start descending and trust that the good stuff is coming. As you continue to move left, you will suddenly arrive in the large chute that is visible from Jay Peak. A prominent 15-foot-wide shot plunges straight downhill for about 100 feet. Enjoy your first of many face shots here. At the bottom of this chute, angle left again, and passageways start to open and close beneath you. This is the magic of Big Jay, where you can find your own personal adventure as you mine this peak for the deepest powder you are likely to find anywhere.

As you continue your descent, you are aimed right at Jay Peak. Take your time and enjoy the ride. Don't descend all the way to the valley floor, which is a brushy drainage. Instead, take a traverse line to the right that is about 150 feet above the valley floor. Keep traversing to the right (south), breaking over the shoulder of Big Jay. You will be bushwhacking (literally) through puckerbrush as you traverse out. Per-

Skiing deep powder on Big Jay. Photo by Kim Brown.

severe—bushwhacking is a character-building rite of passage for eastern mountaineers. It's also the small price you must pay for the fine powder you've just plun-
dered. After bearing right, you finally pick up logging roads that head down toward
VT 242. You will also cross the Catamount Trail, which you can follow to the road.
You come out onto VT 242 about 1.5 miles south of Jay Pass. From here, you can
hitchhike back to the ski area to retrieve your car. And tell your disbelieving friends
about just how deep it can get in the eastern outback.

OTHER OPTIONS

There are several options for more moderate ski tours around Jay Peak. The **Catamount Trail** in this area travels around the lower reaches of Jay Peak and offers
good views of the mountain. *The Catamount Trail Guidebook* (see appendix B) has
a detailed route description.

  Hazen's Notch Cross-Country Ski & Snowshoe Center in Montgomery Center (802-326-4708) offers access to several good ski tours in this area. A scenic
highlight is the ski tour into **Hazen's Notch**. The trail coincides with a busy snowmobile trail for part of the way (avoid it on weekends), but the views are worth it.

MOUNT MANSFIELD REGION

Mount Mansfield (4,393 feet) is the highest mountain in Vermont. Viewed from the east and west, the ridgeline of the mountain resembles the profile of a face. Hence, the names given to the various features along the ridge, from south to north: Forehead, Nose, Upper Lip, Lower Lip, Chin, and Adam's Apple. According the Green Mountain Club *Long Trail Guide*, the Abenaki Indians originally named the mountains Moze-o-de-be-Wadso ("mountain with the head of a moose"). The current name was adopted from the nearby town of Mansfield, which is now defunct.

Mount Mansfield has captured the imagination of skiers since the early 1900s. It was first climbed on skis via the Toll Road on February 1, 1914, by Dartmouth College librarian Nathaniel Goodrich. Goodrich was accompanied by AMC trailsman C. W. Blood, who wore snowshoes. Blood descended the mountain nearly as fast as his skiing partner. Goodrich offered in explanation: "I had a lot of fun, but my stops, voluntary and otherwise, were very frequent."

Numerous ski trails were cut on both sides of Mount Mansfield beginning in the early 1930s. Many of these trails were incorporated into the network of what is now the Stowe Mountain Resort downhill ski area, located on the northeast slopes of the mountain. What the ski area left behind, backcountry skiers can claim today. Mount Mansfield is now home to many of the finest backcountry ski trails in the Northeast. These trails are now cooperatively maintained by the Stowe Mountain Resort and Trapp Family Lodge cross-country ski centers. Much of the history of skiing on Mount Mansfield, and indeed in the U.S., can be found in the storied ski trails described in this section.

The ski tours in the Mount Mansfield region offer a combination of interesting trail skiing and challenging tree skiing. The open forests that remain from the early years of logging activity are now an ideal setting for skiers who enjoy weaving through the birches and finding their own lines of descent. The history of skiing in this area and the quality and variety of ski terrain make this entire region an essential destination for skiers in search of the classic New England skiing experience.

A Note on Maps. The best topographic map that includes all of the ski trails in the Mount Mansfield region, and the Bolton-Trapp Trail, is the excellent *Northern Vermont Adventure Skiing* map by Map Adventures (www.mapadventures.com). This waterproof map is available in stores throughout northern Vermont. The USGS Mount Mansfield quadrangle (1980) does not show the backcountry ski trails.

12
Bruce Trail

THE TOUR

The Bruce Trail plunges 2,000 feet down the south side of Mount Mansfield, ending on the trails of the Stowe Mountain Resort Cross-Country Ski Center. It is a legendary down-mountain ski run cut in the 1930s by the Civilian Conservation Corps.

LENGTH

2.4 miles (Bruce Trail); 4 miles (total tour, Octagon to Stowe Mountain Resort Cross-Country Ski Center)

ELEVATION

Start: 3,640 feet (Octagon)
Finish: 1,100 feet (Stowe Mountain Resort Cross-Country Ski Center)
Vertical drop: 2,540 feet

MAPS

* *Northern Vermont Adventure Skiing* (Map Adventures)
* USGS Mount Mansfield (1980)

DIFFICULTY

Most difficult

SNOWBOARDING

The Bruce Trail is a great backcountry snowboard run. It has a steady downhill grade for most of the way back to the cross-country ski center. A short uphill walk on the cross-country trails is required at the end.

FEE

This ungroomed trail is maintained by the Stowe Mountain Resort Cross-Country Ski Center. If you ride the Forerunner Quad chairlift to the start, you must buy a lift ticket at Stowe Mountain Resort (single-ride tickets are available). If you ski up from the cross-country center, you must purchase a trail pass from the Stowe Mountain Resort Cross-Country Ski Center. There is no charge to ski up the Toll Road, but it is 4 miles to the top of Bruce Trail.

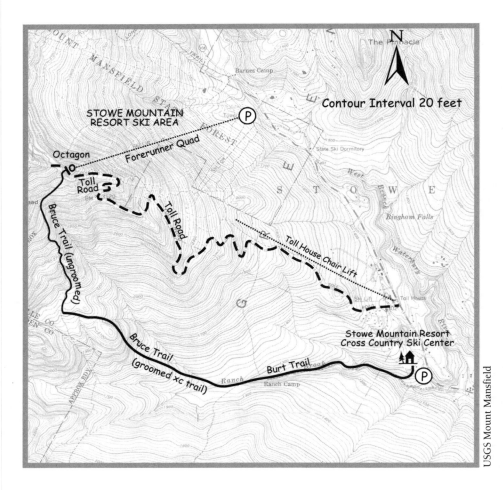

BRUCE TRAIL

HOW TO GET THERE
From Stowe Mountain Resort, take the Forerunner Quad chairlift to the Octagon.
The Bruce Trail leaves from the Toll Road just behind (west of) the Stone Hut.

ADDITIONAL INFORMATION
* Stowe Mountain Resort Cross-Country Ski Center: 802-253-3000,
  www.stowe.com

On June 9, 1933, a contingent of the Civilian Conservation Corps (CCC), the
federal jobs recovery program, arrived in Waterbury, Vermont, just down the
road from Mount Mansfield. Vermont State Forester Perry Merrill, himself an avid
skier, had just the project for these eager young men: He would have them cut a
ski trail from near the summit of Mount Mansfield almost to the Mountain Road
in Stowe. This was the Bruce Trail, named for a well-known local lumberman. It
was the first ski trail on Mount Mansfield.

The Bruce Trail was an immediate hit with skiers. In February 1934 it was
the site of Mount Mansfield's first ski race. The winner was Dartmouth racer Dick
Durrance, who won with a time of 10 minutes, 48 seconds; placing second in that
race was the late Charlie Lord, who directed the CCC in cutting the trail and who
later became the master designer of Mount Mansfield's downhill ski trail system.
The Bruce Trail and the Nose Dive, which descend opposite sides of Mount
Mansfield, were two of the main skiing attractions on the mountain.

The real center of skiing on Mount Mansfield in the early days was a cabin,
not a trail. In 1932, Stowe lumberman and skier Craig Burt Sr. fixed up an old logging camp and turned it into the ski accommodations known as the Ranch Camp.
When Charlie Lord and his CCC contingent were deciding where to cut the Bruce
Trail, they put it where they did in part because it would end at the front door of
the Ranch Camp (which is also where the CCC crew was quartered while they
built the trail). The Ranch Camp was the first headquarters of the Mount
Mansfield Ski Club.

Early skiing on Mount Mansfield was intimately connected with life at the
Ranch Camp. Ski maps of Mount Mansfield from the 1930s show graphically how
the Ranch Camp was a hub, with ski trails radiating from it like the spokes of a
wheel. The camp was located at the junction of the Steeple, Houston, and Bruce
trails—all of which have been recut and restored in recent years, thanks largely to
the efforts of John Higgins, the director of the Stowe Mountain Resort Cross-
Country Ski Center. A sign on the Burt Trail in the cross-country ski center marks
the site today.

Ranch Camp life was the precursor of modern ski bumming. The late Hal
Burton, formerly on the board of directors of the Mount Mansfield Ski Club, once

described to me how the cook at the Ranch Camp "always had a huge iron vat of good New England baked beans on the stove. There were always a lot of very happy skiers inside. We felt privileged to have snow, because there weren't any snowmakers in those days." It cost $1 for three meals and $1 for lodging. There were ultimately three buildings, with bunks for up to forty-four skiers.

Charlie Lord recalled in the early 1970s: "Ranch Camp was a distinctive institution and its clientele really loved to 'get back into the woods.' It had an atmosphere all its own and I suspect that even today it would have appeal, although it probably wouldn't make much money."

The Ranch Camp operated as a ski hut until 1950. Its demise occurred under unfortunate circumstances. In the late 1960s the buildings that comprised the Ranch Camp were occupied by squatters—mostly young hippies who had fled the urban blight. The Burt Lumber Company, which owned the property, disapproved of the situation but the owners were unsure how to handle the problem. They finally opted for a definitive solution: In September 1970 they burned down the buildings. There is now hardly a trace left of the one-time forest enclave of Mount Mansfield skiers.

With the Ranch Camp as a base of operations in the thirties, a 3-mile climb up the Bruce Trail and a run back down was considered a pretty good day. But by

Spring skiing on the Bruce Trail.

1937 the first commercial rope tow had opened on the western slopes of the mountain above the former Mount Mansfield Hotel, and in 1940 a 6,300-foot single chairlift began operation (since replaced by the Forerunner Quad), capable of carrying 200 skiers per hour up the mountain. The Bruce Trail on the undeveloped south side of the mountain was quickly abandoned in favor of the lift-served trails.

The Bruce Trail continued to be skied occasionally by local downhill skiers in the 1950s and 1960s, and locals would periodically cut back the underbrush. In the 1980s and early 1990s, the Bruce became a favorite powder run for telemark skiers, but it was still lightly skied. Today, a boom in interest in adventure skiing and snowboarding has resulted in a new life for the Bruce Trail. The Bruce is now used daily by alpine and telemark skiers and snowboarders, who use it as a lift-serviced backcountry trail. Old-timers who once had this trail to themselves rue the popularity and increased traffic, but this rediscovery merely marks a revival of the spirit of the venerable Bruce Trail. Skiers and riders have come full circle, dusting off this buried treasure to once again appreciate how it shines.

Together with the Teardrop Trail, the Bruce Trail endures as a crown jewel in the CCC's network of down-mountain trails. A ski down the Bruce will make it clear why early skiers traveled so far for this prize.

From the top of the Forerunner Quad chairlift, ski straight ahead to the Stone Hut (where you can stay overnight; contact the Vermont State Ski Dorm at 802-253-4010 for reservations and information). Follow the path to the right at the Stone Hut, then turn left where you emerge on the Toll Road. The Bruce Trail departs from the Toll Road on the right in about 100 feet. The top is unmarked, but there will probably be tracks.

The Bruce Trail starts with a bang: a seven-foot-wide pipeline plunges straight downhill for about 80 feet, then makes an abrupt 90-degree turn to the right. If you survive this initiation, you'll do fine on the rest of the run. The trail then opens up to be about 15 feet wide. It alternately traverses and drops, and is full of quick corners and surprises. Stay on your toes and expect the unexpected. Most of all enjoy the quirky sense of humor of this trail.

There are views of Mount Elmore and the Worcester Mountains to the east as you descend. About a mile down the trail, you turn right and suddenly come upon a sharp horizon line. The short, steep pitch below is the Elevator Shaft, the heart-stopping crux of the run. There is a gentle runout at the bottom of this pitch, just in case you build up too much steam above.

The Bruce Trail has a southeastern exposure, and consequently tends to have less consistent snow conditions than the Teardrop Trail, which has northern and western exposures. It is common to encounter a wide range of snow types when skiing the Bruce, which adds to its interesting personality. Its sunny aspect makes it a friendly place to stop and enjoy the views.

Beyond the Elevator Shaft there are still several miles of turns on more moderate terrain. The Bruce Trail travels through some long, open birch glades before finally coming to a clearly marked intersection with the Overland Trail after 1.1 miles. The Overland climbs up to a pass known as Devil's Dishpan and then descends toward Underhill Center (see the description of this route in the Teardrop Trail section). If you want to extend your tour, you can ski the Overland to the Underhill Trail and return to the Stowe Mountain Resort Cross-Country Ski Center by descending either the Burt or Dewey Trail. This longer tour encompasses every type of skiing, from telemarking down a powder run, to back-country touring, to double-poling or skating your way home on groomed trails.

The Bruce Trail continues straight ahead from its junction with the Overland Trail, ending a mile later at the Burt Trail. The final half-mile of the Bruce is a groomed trail, part of the network of the Stowe Mountain Resort Cross-Country Ski Center. There is another 1.5 miles of groomed skiing on the Burt Trail, at which point you can return to the alpine ski area by following signs saying To Lift, which lead back to the Toll House Double chairlift. Or you may exit at the cross-country center. From there, you can hitchhike the few miles back to your car at the alpine ski area or take one of the Mountain Road shuttle buses.

13

Teardrop Trail

THE TOUR

The Teardrop Trail is a classic down-mountain trail cut in the 1930s by the CCC. It leaves just south of the Nose of Mount Mansfield and descends the steep west face of the mountain.

LENGTH

1.2 miles (to Underhill Trail); 1.8 miles (to Mountain Road, Underhill Center)

ELEVATION

Highest point: 3,900 feet

Bottom: 2,200 feet (Underhill Trail junction); 1,700 feet (Mountain Road)

Vertical drop: 1,700–2,200 feet

MAPS

* *Northern Vermont Adventure Skiing* (Map Adventures)
* USGS Mount Mansfield (1983)

DIFFICULTY

Most difficult

SNOWBOARDING

The Teardrop Trail drops steadily and steeply from start to finish. It is a classic backcountry snowboard run. Snowshoes are needed for the climb up.

HOW TO GET THERE

From Stowe: From Stowe Mountain Resort, take the Forerunner Quad chairlift to the Octagon restaurant (single-ride lift tickets are available). Ski or walk up the Toll Road to the summit, following it past some TV towers until the junction on the right with the Long Trail South (sign). Ski on the Long Trail for 100 yards, passing the Forehead Bypass on the left. Continue straight on the Long Trail; where the hiking trail bends left, you bear right into the woods for about another 100 yards, eventually hitting the top of the Teardrop Trail.

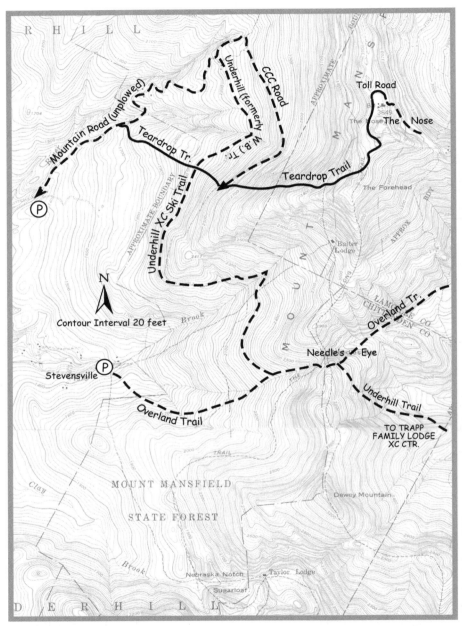

Contour Interval 20 feet

USGS Mount Mansfield

TEARDROP TRAIL

From Underhill Center: From Pleasant Valley Road, turn right onto Mountain Road, drive to where the plowing ends, and park. There are two ways to reach the Teardrop from here: Ski up the unplowed road toward Underhill State Park for about 1 mile. An unmarked trail to the Teardrop departs on the right (east). It connects directly with the bottom of the Teardrop. This is a popular access point for the Teardrop, so there will probably be ski tracks to follow. Alternatively, continue up the unplowed road, passing the gate into Underhill State Park. Ski up the CCC Road, following it to the right (south) at the junction with the Laura Cowles Trail and Sunset Ridge Trail. The junction with the Teardrop Trail is reached 2.1 miles from the park gate.

In 1937, encouraged by the popularity of its ski trails on the Stowe (east) side of Mount Mansfield, the Civilian Conservation Corps (CCC) turned its energies to the "other side" of the mountain. Burlington-area skiers clamored for ski routes on Mansfield that didn't require driving all the way around to Stowe. So the Forest Service issued orders to the CCC to cut a trail that dropped from the summit of Mount Mansfield to the sleepy town of Underhill Center. Stowe's master trail engineer, Charlie Lord, was then serving on the technical staff of the CCC. He laid out the Teardrop Trail, and the CCC trail builders went to work. Perry Merrill gave the trail its name because, as Lord told me before he died in 1997, the trail was so fast "it made tears run from your eyes."

Underhill residents once had visions of a ski development on a par with the alpine ski resort in Stowe. In the late 1930s, slopes were cut on the west side of Mount Mansfield. A 1,000-foot rope tow was installed, and the slopes were lighted for night skiing. Snow trains from New York City would arrive in Burlington, where buses would take them either to Underhill Center or Stowe. "A variety of practice runs, trails which vary in rating from beginner to advanced expert, and the well-known Underhill Ski School combine to make this a Mecca for New York's snowbirds," declared the 1939 guidebook, *Skiing in the East: The Best Trails and How to Get There.* But the Underhill ski scene was eclipsed when the single chairlift began operation in Stowe in 1940. The lift rose 2,000 vertical feet up Mount Mansfield to the Octagon restaurant. The Underhill slopes were the site of several intercollegiate ski meets in the early 1940s, but the operation was abandoned soon after World War II.

The Teardrop was described in one account as "the pièce de résistance" of the trails in the Underhill area. *Skiing in the East* proclaimed it as "one of the most thrilling trails in the East." It originally linked up with a trail to the Halfway House for a total descent of 3 miles. An 800-foot rope tow was at one time in operation at the base of it, along with a warming hut and snack bar.

Despite the quality of this run, the Teardrop never achieved the popularity of the legendary Nose Dive, Chin Clip, and Bruce trails on the "front" side of the mountain. Early Stowe skiers such as Lord, Craig Burt Jr., and the rest of their crowd simply felt it was too much hassle to have to climb up the mountain, ski down the Teardrop, and then climb back up it again to return home. It was left to skiers from Underhill and Burlington to ski and maintain the trail. Ironically, the Teardrop has probably achieved more renown today among telemark skiers than it did in its early years.

What's so special about an abandoned downhill trail that goes down the "wrong" side of the mountain? Its loyal following would agree on one thing: powder. While weekend warriors may be scraping their way down the hard-packed slopes at the ski area, backcountry skiers and riders are floating through knee-deep fluff on the "back" side. The Teardrop is usually a reliable powder stash even when snow in the lowlands is sparse.

Like many CCC ski trails, the Teardrop has a distinctive personality. Turns were placed strategically to keep the route interesting and challenging, and the trail moves with the terrain contours. The Teardrop banks, dips, turns, and rolls right along with the mountain, staying unpredictable throughout its entire length. Just as importantly, the trail was located where the snow dumped heavily and lasted longest. There were no snowmakers or groomers seventy years ago to replenish the trail after a day's ski, so skiers had to place the trail where Mother Nature could help.

Skiing the Teardrop still presents a logistical challenge. Shuttling a car so as to avoid climbing back up the trail is impractical: it is nearly a 50-mile drive all the way around Mount Mansfield from Stowe to Underhill Center. The sensible solution is to start and finish on the same side of the mountain. If you are skiing from Underhill Center, climb the Teardrop from the bottom and descend the same way. From Stowe, take the Forerunner Quad chairlift and hike to top of the Teardrop, then ski or ride down the trail and climb back out. Return to your car by skiing down one of the ski area trails. A third option is ambitious but aesthetic: start from Stowe and ski the Teardrop as part of an around-the-mountain ski tour. But first, some details on skiing the Teardrop.

The Teardrop originally started from the Nose Dive Trail, which at one time extended all the way to the top of the Nose (this abandoned top section of the Nose Dive is still visible as a brushy trail that continues uphill from the current start of Nose Dive). Today, the start of the Teardrop is intentionally discreet and difficult to find. Local skiers have left the start of the trail obscure in the hope of keeping skier traffic down. Despite this well-intentioned effort, the Teardrop is no longer a local secret. The trail is heavily skied, especially on weekends. But the fact that the word is out about the Teardrop has not diminished its appeal. It is still wide and powdery enough that a number of skiers and riders can find their own untracked lines.

Telemarking down the Teardrop Trail.

The most difficult section of the Teardrop is the very top. A narrow chute threads among stunted trees, and this section is often windblown and icy. But the trail opens steadily into a 20-foot-wide swath heading west. The trail slabs across the north side of a buttress that runs from the Forehead. There is a double fall line to contend with for the first half of the run. Looking back up the trail there is an impressive view of the cliffy western face of the Forehead.

The Teardrop begins with a gradual traverse, then starts snapping back and forth across the fall line. Right-angle turns force you to keep swooping around blind corners while the trail twists downhill. Steep drops alternate with some gradual run-outs, with barely enough time to catch your breath in between. Skiing the Teardrop evokes the same sensation as paddling a good whitewater run: you drift slowly through a calm section, get lured unwittingly into the next chute, pick up speed, then work the subtle currents in the river as you fly down the big drops. The Zen of negotiating all these forms of white water is the same: stay centered, relaxed, and balanced. Move with the terrain, not against it. Go with the flow.

The Teardrop descends quickly, and after 1 mile it intersects with the CCC Road. The Teardrop jogs left about 30 yards, then continues downhill for another 0.2 mile. This lower section begins with the steepest drop yet, descending a sometimes-bony headwall. The official trail then peters out in open forest, allowing you to end the run with some great tree skiing. If you are parked on the Mountain Road in Underhill Center, continue down on a trail through the forest for another half-mile to reach the road and your car.

The Teardrop covers a full range of downhill skiing terrain, from narrow chutes, to open powder skiing, to tighter tree shots. You can pull out all the stops on the Teardrop and try everything in your bag of tricks. The action-packed variety is what makes this trail so interesting and fun to ski.

The Teardrop has developed a loyal following among local skiers. It has gone from being a historical relic to a trail where skiers vie with one another to claim first tracks after a storm. The passions that this route inspires are understandable: when conditions are right, it is one of the best powder runs in New England.

AROUND-THE-MOUNTAIN TOUR

The Around-the-Mountain Tour is the most adventurous—and the longest—way to complete a run down the Teardrop Trail. The idea is to nearly circumnavigate Mount Mansfield. From the bottom of the Teardrop, you can ski back all the way around the mountain to finish at the Stowe Mountain Resort Cross-Country Ski Center, which is just down the road from the alpine ski area.

The Teardrop officially ends at a junction with what was formerly called the W. B. Trail, renamed in 1999 the Underhill Trail. (NOTE: Older maps label this north-south trail the W. B. Trail, and refer to what is now called the Overland Trail from Stevensville to the Devil's Dishpan as the Underhill Trail. Making matters more confusing, there is another Underhill Trail that runs east from Devil's Dish-pan to Rob George Saddle). This junction is marked only by orange plastic blazes and is easy to miss. Turning right (north) on the Underhill Trail brings you back to the CCC Road and the parking lot in Underhill State Park. Turning left (south) on the Underhill Trail will begin the Around-the-Mountain Tour.

The Underhill Trail leads gradually uphill for 2 miles and is presently sparse-ly blazed and poorly maintained. It crosses the Butler Lodge Trail and ends at the Overland Trail (formerly the Underhill Trail), where you turn left. In 0.3 mile, the Overland Trail ends at the Needles Eye. (NOTE: *Northern Vermont Adventure Ski-ing* map incorrectly shows the Needles Eye next to Butler Lodge. Its correct loca-tion is next to Devil's Dishpan).

The Needles Eye is an imposing rock cleft that divides the long Mount Mans-field ridge. The Overland Trail skirts the Needles Eye by cutting right (south), passing over the col known as the Devil's Dishpan. The Overland drops quickly at first as it descends a narrow drainage, but it soon flattens out as it approaches its junction with the lower section of the Bruce Trail in 0.7 mile. Turning right (east) on the Bruce leads to the Burt Trail, part of the trail system of the Stowe Mountain Resort Cross-Country Ski Center. The Burt Trail ends at the cross-country center on the Mountain Road.

The total distance for the Around-the-Mountain Tour is nearly 7 miles (including the Teardrop). Start early, and expect to take a full day to complete the tour. The Underhill Trail can be difficult to follow, and you may be breaking trail for some or all of the tour. Getting back to your car in daylight is always a nice bonus.

14

Skytop Trail

THE TOUR

A high elevation ridge trail with spectacular views of Mount Mansfield and the surrounding peaks. It connects a number of ungroomed backcountry ski trails of the Trapp Family Lodge and Stowe Mountain Resort cross-country ski centers.

LENGTH

* 2.8 miles (Skytop Trail, Rob George Saddle to Dewey Saddle)
* Total length of ski tour when starting from Trapp Family Lodge: 9.8 miles; from Stowe Mountain Resort Cross-Country Ski Center: 8.3 miles

ELEVATION

Start: 1,100 feet (Stowe Mountain Resort Cross-Country Ski Center); 1,350 feet (Trapp Family Lodge)

Highest point: 2,980 feet

Vertical drop: 1,630 feet (Trapp's); 1,880 feet (Stowe)

MAPS

* *Northern Vermont Adventure Skiing* (Map Adventures)
* USGS Bolton Mountain (1983) shows the terrain but not this trail.

DIFFICULTY

Moderate/more difficult

FEE

The Skytop Trail is part of the backcountry trail network of the Trapp Family Lodge Cross-Country Ski Center, which is jointly maintained by Stowe Mountain Resort. The trail can be reached from the Trapp Family Lodge, the Stowe Mountain Resort Cross-Country Ski Center, or the Topnotch Cross-Country Ski Center. You must purchase a trail pass from the cross-country center where you begin.

HOW TO GET THERE

The Stowe Mountain Resort Cross-Country Ski Center and the Topnotch Resort Cross-Country Ski Center are located on the Mountain Road in Stowe. The

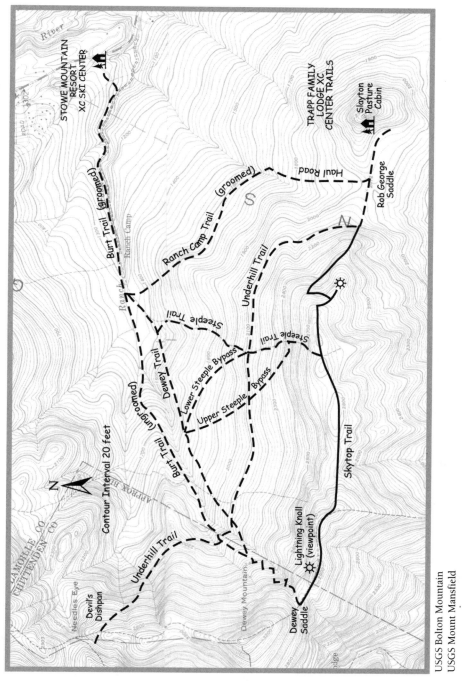

SKYTOP TRAIL

USGS Bolton Mountain
USGS Mount Mansfield

Trapp Family Lodge Cross-Country Ski Center is located off Luce Hill Road in Stowe. See below for trail directions.

ADDITIONAL INFORMATION

✳ Stowe Mountain Resort Cross-Country Ski Center: 802-253-3000, www.stowe.com

✳ Trapp Family Lodge Cross-Country Ski Center: 802-253-8511, www.trappfamilylodge.com

The Skytop Trail is one of the prettiest ski tours in Vermont. The trail follows a 1.6-mile-long ridge that lies in the heart of the rugged Mount Mansfield region. Traveling along the lee side of the ridge, it is common to find fresh powder on Skytop even when snow is sparse in the valleys below. With its knolls, hollows, and high clearings, Skytop is a romantic world unto itself, a place to retreat to from the madding crowds.

The Skytop Trail offers pristine forest skiing at a high elevation with superb views—ideal attributes for a backcountry tour. Add to this its relatively easy access: it can be reached from three of the four cross-country ski centers in Stowe. All of this combines to make the Skytop Trail an excellent introduction to backcountry skiing. A trip to Skytop is sure to make skiers at the cross-country centers wish they had been wandering off-piste much sooner.

The Skytop Trail was cut by the Burt Lumber Company in the late 1930s. It was originally used by skiers who wanted to make a loop trip from the Ranch Camp, the fabled skier's retreat located in what is now the Stowe Mountain Resort Cross-Country Ski Center, to the Conway Trail (now the Burt Trail). Craig Burt Sr., owner of the Burt Lumber Company, was an important force in the expansion of skiing in the Mount Mansfield area. He was known as the "father of Stowe skiing." Burt was an avid skier himself, although by the account of his son, Craig Burt Jr., he was no expert. His son described to me how his father used to go ski touring with his 8-foot-long double-grooved wood skis and one pole, which he used to brake with. "His idea of fun was to take his skis, one ski pole, and a shotgun and go out for a rabbit hunt," recalls Burt. "He would bushwhack around, but he seldom came home with a rabbit."

The elder Burt had his loggers open up trails in areas where they had already put logging roads. He wanted to link up existing roads and trails to create a large network on which skiers could spend a full day touring. He was partly motivated by the fact that his sons were enthusiastic skiers. Burt was responsible for a number of other ski trails and related developments, including the Ranch Camp (see the Bruce Trail chapter for this history) and he provided the logging roads on which the Bruce Trail begins.

Kicking and gliding through the forest along the Skytop Trail.

When Johannes von Trapp began looking into the prospects for opening up a lodge and cross-country ski center in the Mount Mansfield valley in the 1960s, it occurred to him that the abandoned 1930s-era ski trails would be perfect for developing again. In the spring of 1969, he climbed up to the Skytop ridge and went in search of the old blazes. He found most of them, and even came across an old first aid cache in the Dewey Saddle. Von Trapp says that he tried to have the new Skytop Trail follow the old route as much as possible. He credits the high quality of the wilderness trails in today's Trapp Family Lodge network to the fact that Craig Burt Sr. was so meticulous in the way he cut logging roads. These woods roads were well leveled and cut with a moderate grade so they could be negotiated by oxen and horses.

Your first decision on this ski tour is to decide in which direction you want to ski the Skytop loop. The fastest approach is to climb on groomed trails from either Stowe Mountain Resort or Trapp's. This brings you to the Rob George Saddle, from where you would ski the trail from east to west. Descending the Burt Trail from Dewey Saddle is a fun, steep and twisty run; this is the most challenging section of the tour. Alternatively, you can climb the Burt Trail and ski Skytop from west to east to Rob George Saddle. Approaching this way usually takes up to an hour longer, but you can enjoy the solitude of climbing on backcountry trails. Finally, you can simply ski out Skytop as far as you like, then turn around and backtrack the way you came. Either way, skiing the full Skytop Trail takes most of a very pleasant day.

To reach Skytop from the Trapp Family Lodge, ski to the Slayton Pasture Cabin (a good place to stop for a last hot chocolate), then follow the Cabin Trail a short distance to the Rob George Saddle (2.6 miles). The saddle, named for the farmer who once lived there, is a large clearing with views of all the surrounding peaks. The Skytop Trail leaves off to the left (as you look at Mount Mansfield). The trail quickly enters the forest and begins to climb steadily on old woods roads. Make note of what lies downhill of the switchback turns if you plan to come back the same way. If there is a light snow cover, this section has a number of drainage divots to beware of on the descent. After a mile of climbing, the trail turns sharply south and begins to contour until it reaches the long ridge that gives the tour its character, as well as its name. A sign indicates a scenic vista at the beginning of the ridge, where there are views to the south of Camel's Hump.

If you are starting at the Stowe Mountain Resort Cross-Country Ski Center, ski up to Rob George Saddle via the Ranch Camp Trail and the Haul Road. For the longer tour, climb on either the Burt Trail or the Dewey Trail to Dewey Saddle (3.3 miles), from where you climb up to Lightning Knoll and take in views of the whole Ranch Valley on the south side of Mount Mansfield.

The Skytop Trail travels on rolling terrain between 2,800 and 2,900 feet along the top of the ridge. The trail meanders around small knolls and snakes its way through white and yellow birches. The forested ridge refracts the southern light, throwing zebralike stripes across the snow and the forest floor. The feeling up here is quiet and magical. Moose, deer, and other animals prance around freely on the ridge, unaccustomed to seeing people.

If you are skiing east to west, note a caution sign on a tree just past Lightning Knoll. This is your only warning that you are about to drop steeply on a narrow trail into Dewey Saddle, the col that separates Dewey Mountain from the Skytop ridge. The saddle marks the end of the Skytop Trail and the start of the Burt Trail.

Skiing down the Burt Trail is a thrilling telemark run through an open hardwood forest. Formerly called the Conway Trail, this was a popular down-mountain ski trail that led to the Ranch Camp. Conway was the name of a former logging camp in the Ranch Valley. The Burt Trail soon comes to a junction with the Dewey Trail and the Underhill Trail. The Dewey offers the option of a slightly longer ungroomed downhill run back to the Stowe Mountain Resort Cross-Country Ski Center. Beware of stream crossings lower down on both the Dewey and the Burt trails.

Your options for returning to the Trapp Family Lodge Cross-Country Ski Center include backtracking on the Skytop Trail, which ends with an enjoyable, wide downhill trail descending from the ridge back to the Rob George Saddle. Or you can make a loop trip by descending the Burt Trail, then returning on the Underhill Trail, which is basically flat for the 2.7-mile ski back to the Rob George Saddle. All junctions are clearly marked with trail signs.

15

Steeple Trail

THE TOUR

A thrilling, steep descent of a classic, winding 1930s-era ski trail in the shadow of Mount Mansfield.

LENGTH

1.2 miles

ELEVATION

Start/highest point: 2,800 feet
Finish: 1,400 feet
Vertical drop: 1,400 feet

MAPS

* *Northern Vermont Adventure Skiing* (Map Adventures)
* USGS Bolton Mountain (1983) and USGS Mount Mansfield (1983)

DIFFICULTY

Upper Steeple: Most difficult; Lower Steeple: More difficult

FEE

The Steeple can be reached via the groomed trails of one of three Stowe cross-country centers: Stowe Mountain Resort, Trapp Family Lodge, or Topnotch. You must purchase a trail pass where you begin this tour.

SNOWBOARDING

The Steeple runs continuously downhill for its entire length and is a good snowboard descent. The fastest approach/exit is to take the groomed Burt Trail back to the Stowe Mountain Resort Cross-Country Ski Center (1.5 miles). This has a gentle downhill grade. Snowshoes, which are allowed on the groomed cross-country center trails, are needed for the climb. When snowshoeing up the backcountry ski trails, take care to walk next to the ski tracks, not in them.

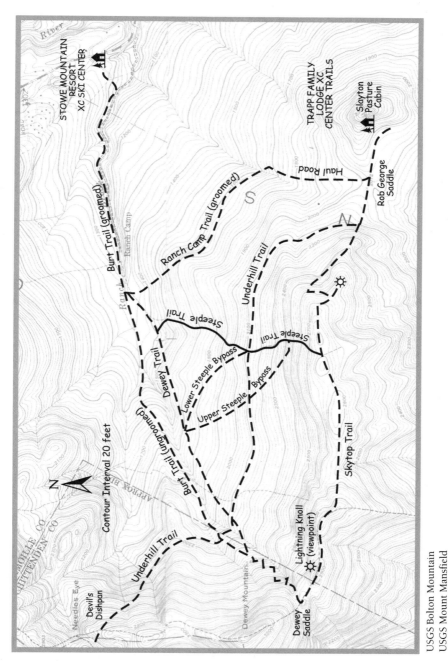

STEEPLE TRAIL

HOW TO GET THERE

The fastest access to the Steeple is from the Stowe Mountain Resort Cross-Country Ski Center. The center is located on the Mountain Road in Stowe.

ADDITIONAL INFORMATION

✻ Stowe Mountain Resort Cross-Country Ski Center: 802-253-3000, www.stowe.com

If you mention "Stowe" and "steeple," most people naturally assume you are referring to the stately whitewashed tower of the Stowe Community Church, which has stood watch over the town since 1863. But for skiers in search of a religious experience, the "Steeple" they have long sought in Stowe is a fabulous, steep, powder-choked trail that resides high in the Ranch Valley. This is the Steeple Trail, one of the Vermont's earliest, and still among its best, backcountry downhill ski trails.

The Steeple was cut by volunteers in 1937 at the same time as the Perry Merrill Trail, which is still in use today as an alpine ski trail within Stowe Mountain Resort. The Steeple was intended to expand the variety of ski offerings around Mount Mansfield. All the new ski trails were linked, so as to make for interesting and varied ski touring. A 1938 article in *The Ski Bulletin* about skiing in Stowe explained:

"Since the Trails Committee [of the Mount Mansfield Ski Club] has made an effort to take advantage of as many connections as possible and to develop circular routes, most of the trails are interconnected.... The Trails Committee developed its work with the purpose of meeting three needs: first, an outstanding down-mountain racing trail, such as the Nose Dive, and a jump; second, a system of trails that intermediate skiers would find interesting, yet within their ability; and third, trails for skiers who add to their skiing the love of photography or of the all-day trip." Thus, many of the ski tours around Mount Mansfield were intentionally designed as ambitious outings. People had come a long way to ski at Stowe, and to them a good ski tour was a full-day event. There were plans to link the trails of the Ranch Valley with Bolton Mountain (since achieved with the Bolton-Trapp Trail), and to extend trails all the way north to Morristown.

The Steeple, along with the Bruce Trail, started right from the Ranch Camp, a rustic cabin used as a base for adventuring by Mount Mansfield's earliest ski bums (see the Bruce Trail chapter for a history of the Ranch Camp). The Steeple rose 1,300 feet to where it met the Skytop Trail. *The Ski Bulletin* announced in 1938 that "the Steeple Trail is not designed as a racing trail, but is a fast run requiring controlled skiing." A 1939 ski guidebook described the Steeple as "a fast run with excellent scenic effect. The upper half-mile is very steep and trees have been left in several places, making controlled skiing a necessity." It was rated as an "expert and intermediate" run.

There are several explanations about how the trail got its name. By one account, skiers thought it was "steeper than hell," or "like the side of a steeple." Another version of the story is that the peak it descends was once called Steeple Mountain.

By the 1950s, the Steeple had vanished into the forest. The problem was that the Steeple required skiers to "earn their turns": the only way to ski it was to climb it, just as the first skiers did. The Bruce Trail, by contrast, could be reached by a chairlift. As a result, the Bruce has been maintained over the years by loyal back-country skiers. The Steeple, and the tithe of sweat equity that it required of its devotees, disappeared.

In the mid-1990s, the Steeple rose from the dead. The people responsible for this miracle were John Higgins and Jeff Baldwin, the director and head groomer, respectively, of the Stowe Mountain Resort Cross-Country Ski Center. The two men, joined by local volunteers, found and recut the Steeple. Higgins, a ski history buff, says his motivation was simple. "We wanted to ski it," he declares. "We had always skied off the Skytop Ridge. We had heard about the Steeple, but we didn't know where it went." Friends of his dismissed his notion that there was an old down-mountain trail there, and bet him a case of beer that it didn't exist. Sufficiently intrigued and motivated, Higgins found old maps, and then he and Baldwin rediscovered some of the old trail blazes on the trees. He won his bet, and restored a great ski run to boot. Higgins and Baldwin have also been responsible for restoring the Houston Trail, which runs from the Toll Road to the old Ranch Camp site, and for recutting the Dewey Trail (formerly the Edson Dewey), which parallels the Burt Trail almost to the Dewey Saddle. This labor of love by these latter day trailblazers has restored the seventy-year-old luster to the Ranch Valley. It is once again a thriving hub of backcountry skiing in the East.

There are many options for how to reach the Steeple Trail, but all of them require an investment of time and effort. You can choose to ski the entire run or only a section of it. The best approach to the Steeple is from the Stowe Mountain Resort Cross-Country Ski Center. The center maintains the trail, and the staff has the most up-to-date information on trail conditions.

The top of the Steeple leaves from the Skytop Trail. From the Stowe Mountain Resort Cross-Country Ski Center, head out on the groomed Burt Trail, skiing alongside the scenic Ranch Brook. After 1.5 miles you reach a major trail junction, where you can choose your route. The fastest approach to the top of the Steeple is to ski up the groomed Ranch Camp Trail, eventually turning right onto the Haul Road, which is part of the trail system of the Trapp Family Lodge Cross-Country Ski Center. The Haul Road delivers you to the Rob George Saddle, where you can pick up the ungroomed Skytop Trail (see the Skytop Trail chapter for details) to

Weaving through the birch trees on the Steeple Trail.

reach the top of the Steeple. Total distance from the Burt Trail junction to the top of the Steeple via the Rob George Saddle is 3 miles.

The Steeple can also be skied in shorter pieces. From the Rob George Saddle, you can ski on the ungroomed Underhill Trail for 1.3 miles, where you come to a junction with the Lower Steeple. This eliminates skiing the steepest upper one-third of the Steeple. You can also reach this Lower Steeple junction by skiing from the Stowe Mountain Resort Cross-Country Center on the Dewey Trail. From the Burt Trail, ski 0.8 mile up the Dewey to a three-way junction with the Lower Steeple Cutoff and the Upper Steeple Cutoff. The Lower Steeple Cutoff joins the Lower Steeple at the Underhill Trail. The Upper Steeple Cutoff connects with the Steeple at 2,400 feet, just below the headwall near the top of the trail. The Upper Steeple is a steep climb; it is best skied as a downhill variation when starting from the top of the Steeple.

Finally, consider skiing the Steeple as part of a scenic "grand tour" of the Ranch Valley. From the Burt Trail junction, continue all the way up either the Burt or Dewey Trail (they rejoin higher up) to Dewey Saddle. Pick up the western end of the Skytop Trail here, and ski it east until it meets the Steeple Trail. Total distance from the Burt Trail junction to the top of the Steeple via this route is 3.3 miles.

Starting from the Skytop Trail, the Steeple draws you in slowly. It starts to weave downhill through tall old birch trees, steadily picking up speed. Suddenly, the trail narrows and drops off precipitously onto a steep headwall. This section is stumpy and rocky, and needs a good deal of snow to be skiable. Climbing straight up the Steeple is not recommended, since you will likely scrape off the snow that you plan to ski in this section. Below the headwall, the Upper Steeple Cutoff enters at a two-story rock, and the Steeple Trail jogs to the right. The Steeple stays in the fall line but eases off here, and you can take more leisurely turns through the trees. Giant old birches are sprinkled all along this trail for you to carve turns around. You soon cross the Underhill Trail, where the Lower Steeple Cutoff joins. Below here, the Lower Steeple moderates, but there are plenty of turns yet to come. A solid snowplow with a few good turns to check your speed should suffice on this section. John Higgins recut the trail leaving plenty of trees, making this lower section an enjoyable low-angle glade. You finally return to the Burt Trail junction, where other cross-country skiers may ogle you curiously, wondering why you are covered in snow and smiling from ear to ear.

The Steeple is a thrilling classic run that alternately hurtles and rolls down the mountain. Throughout the tour, you are treated to nice views over the Ranch Valley and to the Green Mountains beyond. The prize of the Steeple is reserved for those who invest the effort required to reach it. Once you ski it, you will undoubtedly become another one of the faithful.

16

Nebraska Notch

THE TOUR

A ski tour into the dramatic and scenic Nebraska Notch. The tour can be done from either Stevensville or Moscow.

LENGTH

* 4.4 miles round-trip (Stevensville trailhead to Taylor Lodge)
* 3.2 miles round-trip (Lake Mansfield Trout Club to Taylor Lodge)

ELEVATION

Start: 1,400 feet (Stevensville); 1,200 feet (Moscow)

Highest point: 1,800 feet

Vertical drop: 400–600 feet

MAPS

* *Northern Vermont Adventure Skiing* (Map Adventures)
* USGS Bolton Mountain (1983)

DIFFICULTY

Moderate (from Stevensville); more difficult/most difficult (from Moscow)

HOW TO GET THERE

From Underhill Center: Drive 0.6 mile north and turn right on Stevensville Road, which you follow for 1.6 miles until the road turns sharply left at a sign for the Maple Leaf Farm. Drive directly ahead (east) here, continuing straight on a dirt road for 1 mile until you reach the parking lot for the Nebraska Notch Trail. *Warning:* The 1-mile road to the trailhead parking lot is very narrow, goes uphill, and is often icy. Do not attempt this road in bad conditions unless you are confident that your vehicle can make it. In any case, it's a good idea to have a shovel and tow cable in your car. Many cars get stuck here!

   Note: Signs for a skier's parking lot at the bottom of the road, and signs at the trailhead warning that you will be towed, are misleading. The Nebraska Notch trailhead is a legal parking lot that is plowed and maintained by the state. Do not block any driveways, however, or you may indeed be towed. If the trailhead

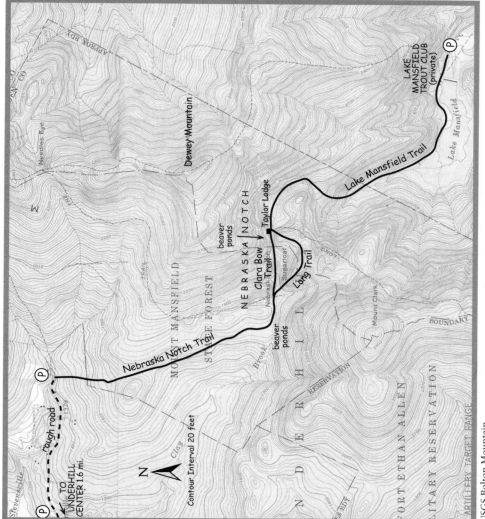

NEBRASKA NOTCH

USGS Bolton Mountain
USGS Mount Mansfield

parking lot is full, you will have to park at the lower skier's parking lot next to Stevensville Road, which will necessitate a 1-mile walk back to the trailhead.

From Moscow: From VT 100 just south of Stowe village, turn onto Moscow Road and continue straight on it as it becomes Nebraska Valley Road. There is a plowed parking pullout at the end of Nebraska Valley Road next to the gate for the Lake Mansfield Trout Club (take care not to block the gate or road here). There is also a skier's parking lot on Old County Road, from which it is a 0.4-mile ski back to the trailhead at the Trout Club.

Nebraska Notch is the east-west passage between Mount Clark (2,979 feet) and Dewey Mountain (3,371 feet). It is an exceptionally pretty area, one of those gems you occasionally stumble across in your travels through the mountains that keep drawing you back for years. At one time a road passed through the notch, allowing passage from Stevensville to Moscow. It was a rough winter road that was eventually abandoned, the only trace of it being the ski and hiking trail described here.

According to one local inn owner, "In most places, people cut roads up the valleys. But in Vermont, there was always some guy who had a girlfriend over the next ridge, so he cut a road over the top of the mountain." If that is the case, the labor of a lovelorn Vermonter is now a plum for skiers. This ski tour is a perfect day trip, combining classic Vermont vistas with fun woods skiing.

The tour can be done either from Stevensville (part of Underhill Center), or Moscow (part of Stowe). The ski tour is shorter but more challenging from Moscow.

From the trailhead in Stevensville, a sign directs you to the right for the trail to Taylor Lodge. The trail forks after 0.2 mile; the Overland Trail (formerly the Underhill Trail) is the trail heading off left, while the Nebraska Notch trail leaves right. Both trails are marked with blue blazes. The Nebraska Notch Trail rises gently through open hardwoods. Just before reaching a large beaver pond, the trail passes through a long, open birch glade, which is an irresistible tree-skiing romp on the way down.

At the east end of the beaver ponds, there is a trail junction. The Clara Bow Trail continues straight ahead, while the Long Trail proceeds right for 0.4 mile to Taylor Lodge. The Clara Bow Trail, described as "rough" on the sign, is a drainage strewn with house-sized boulders. The trail is among the wildest in the state: you scramble among the boulders, and at one point you must climb a short ice-encrusted ladder out of a cave! The Clara Bow trail is sparsely blazed and difficult to follow.

Alternatively, follow the well-marked Long Trail to the right. The LT climbs up and over a col and drops suddenly to the three-sided wooden shelter main-

A quiet winter day in Nebraska Notch.

tained by the Green Mountain Club. Taylor Lodge was constructed in 1978 and named for James P. Taylor, the founder of the Green Mountain Club. It is a spacious shelter that includes a porch, picnic tables, a loft, and sleeping room for fifteen. The picturesque setting and the easy access make the lodge a good destination for a ski camping trip. From Taylor Lodge, there is a view of Lake Mansfield below and the Skytop ridge up to the northeast. The Nebraska Valley is the only glacial cirque in Vermont and has long attracted the attention of geologists. Lake Mansfield itself is man-made, the dam having originally been built to enhance local fishing.

The approach to Nebraska Notch from Moscow is more direct but steeper. The Lake Mansfield Trail begins at a gate for the Lake Mansfield Trout Club, which is closed in winter. The trail is well marked and bears right around the Trout Club buildings. The trail soon emerges out onto the north shore of Lake Mansfield. The lake forms a trackless white canvas with the rolling ridgeline of the Nebraska Valley framing it. At the north end of the lake, the trail bears right; look uphill to see a fence and a green trail sign. Note that this area is well posted, with the intent to keep skiers and hikers off the Trout Club land.

At 1,400 feet, the Lake Mansfield Trail begins a short steep ascent. Ice-covered cliffs lie on the south side of the small valley. The trail soon levels out and parallels a beautiful canyonlike drainage. Deep rock walls rise up on the left, but this view is quickly replaced as the trail turns sharply left to arrive at a large beaver pond. The ice-plastered walls of Nebraska Notch tower overhead. Ski out onto the frozen beaver ponds to take in the remarkable views. If you skied to Taylor Lodge from Stevensville, you should ski down onto the floor of Nebraska Notch to fully appreciate its grandeur.

Nebraska Notch is a primeval place. Stunted tree trunks stick up out of the white expanse of the beaver ponds. Black rock walls striped with fangs of ice soar overhead. Dull blue ice pours down from the summit of Dewey Mountain. It appears that the earth has been cleaved open to reveal its bowels here. The valley floor is dotted with glacial erratics that lie willy-nilly, as if hurled from the side of the mountain by some angry giant. On a sunny day, small ice avalanches cascade down the cliff. Birds shriek maniacally, streaking low across the valley bottom and then soaring upward on thermals. This is an otherworldly place that is all the more dramatic in its winter guise.

The Lake Mansfield Trail back to the Trout Club has one brief steep and narrow section of challenging skiing. If you prefer, you can walk this section, as the trail is typically well packed by hikers and snowshoers. The rest of the trail is a pleasant glide back to the floor of the Nebraska Valley.

The descent from Taylor Lodge to Stevensville can be skied on the trail or through the open trees. This sets the tone for the rest of the ride down: ski it as you see it. There is good open forest skiing for nearly the entire distance back to the trailhead. This is a delightful, moderate downhill run on which you can link turns at your own pace, and discover for yourself why Vermont skiers are so enamored of "skiing the trees."

NEW YORK

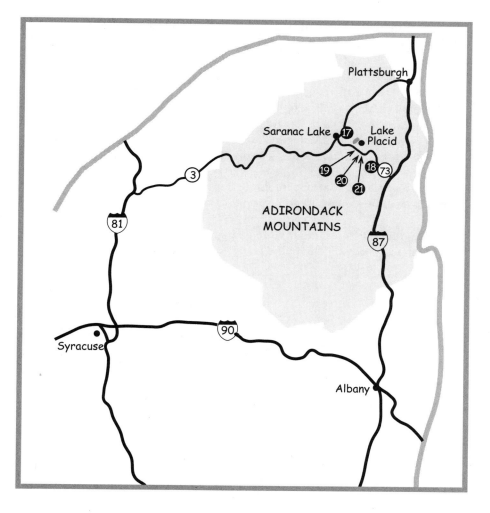

17. Jackrabbit Trail
18. Camp Peggy O'Brien Hut Tour
19. Wright Peak Ski Trail
20. Avalanche Pass
21. Mount Marcy

A NOTE ON MAPS

There are two widely available topographical maps that cover the High Peaks of the Adirondacks:

The Adirondack Mountain Club* (800-395-8080, www.adk.org) publishes *Trails of the Adirondack High Peaks*, which has a distinctive brown shading. This map covers the mountain region between Lake Placid and Elizabethtown. The Club also publishes a full set of maps covering other parts of the Adirondacks. ADK maps are frequently revised and are the most reliable reference.

Adirondack Maps (518-576-9861, www.adirondackmaps.com) publishes the 34" x 44" green shaded map, *The Adirondacks: High Peaks Region*. This map covers from Paul Smiths to Elizabethtown, and is available in many convenience stores in the area. Adirondack Maps also publishes maps covering other parts of the Adirondacks, but many of these maps have not been revised since the 1980s.

Dates given for USGS topographical maps in the following chapters refer to the most recent revision or photo inspection.

Note: The Adirondack Mountain Club is commonly referred to as the "ADK," and this term appears occasionally in the text.

THE ADIRONDACKS
A Ski History

The Adirondack Mountains are one of the greatest ranges of the East. The mountains lie within the 6-million-acre Adirondack State Park, the largest park in the continental U.S. Those who journey to the top of New York will immediately sense that this region is distinctly different from the Green Mountains of Vermont and the White Mountains of New Hampshire. The Adirondacks comprise a majestic, almost incongruous landscape. In contrast to the softly rounded glacial domes that characterize most summits in New England, the jagged Adirondack skyline appears strikingly alpine. There are the Wolfjaw Mountains gaping skyward like a hungry animal. Giant Mountain with a huge eagle-shaped slide torn into its east face. Gothics, its towering flanks raked by rock slides. And Mount Marcy, the crown jewel of New York, capping the state like an enormous ice-cream cone.

The Adirondacks are, in fact, unique: They are the only mountains in the eastern U.S. not geologically part of the Appalachian chain, which extends from Maine to Georgia. The Adirondacks form part of the Canadian Shield, an area of igneous and metamorphic rock that underlies about half of Canada. The mountains are young by geological standards; indeed, mountain formation is still underway here. Earthquakes occur with some regularity. Large new landslides periodically tear a hole in the green carpet that covers the mountains. Avalanches occasionally race down the steepest slopes. This is a living landscape that is constantly changing.

The Adirondacks have an unusual political status. In 1885, the New York state legislature created the Adirondack Forest Preserve with the stipulation that it "shall be forever kept as wild forest lands." In 1892, the legislature created the Adirondack State Park, which included the forest preserve plus all privately owned land within a somewhat arbitrarily drawn "blue line" (for the blue pencil used to indicate the area on the state map). In 1894, responding to environmental abuses, New Yorkers voted to incorporate the "forever wild" clause into the state constitution. The Adirondacks thus became the only wildlands in the country that enjoy such constitutional protection. This strict control has also brought some headaches, as skiers have discovered when they have tried to cut or maintain trails wide enough to ski on (as it has been interpreted, the law prohibits the cutting of mountain trails wider than about 10 feet).

SKIING IN THE ADIRONDACKS

The first skier known to have passed through the Adirondacks was a John Booth of Ottawa. He arrived in Saranac Lake in 1892 to visit his daughter, who was being treated for tuberculosis. A major impetus for skiing came with the opening of the Lake Placid Club in 1904. The club, according to its brochure, was "an informal university in the wilderness, a meeting and working area that combined civilization with leisure and beauty, access to the vitalizing forces of nature, and contact with many of those contributing to the nation's growth." The Lake Placid Club was to bring a number of European ski instructors over who led trips into the mountains. This firmly established skiing as a pastime in the Adirondacks, at least for its blue-blooded clientele.

Two of the early pioneers of Adirondack skiing were Irving Langmuir and John S. Apperson, both of whom worked for General Electric in Schenectady. Langmuir, who is best known as the winner of the 1932 Nobel Prize for chemistry, began skiing the northeastern peaks in 1906, becoming the first major ski mountaineer in North America. In 1907 he skied the Wittenberg in the Catskills, and the following year he skied up Mount Greylock in Massachusetts. Langmuir met Apperson in 1910 and the two men became fast friends. Langmuir shared his enthusiasm for skiing with Apperson, while Apperson introduced Langmuir to the Adirondacks.

Apperson made the first ski ascent of Mount Marcy in 1911 with two other partners. Apperson and Langmuir continued to pioneer routes throughout the Adirondacks. They skied Gothics in 1927, and Apperson is credited with the first ski ascent of Basin and Saddleback mountains that year.

A milestone in Adirondack skiing came in 1912, when the famous Arctic explorer Fridtjof Nansen came to Lake Placid with his daughter. Being Scandinavian, they opted to tour around on skis, rather than the snowshoes favored by most people in the area. Nansen and his daughter spent Christmas at Lake Placid and then climbed Whiteface Mountain, a feat that amazed many locals.

The man who made the biggest impact on Adirondack skiing was Herman Smith "Jackrabbit" Johannsen. Born in Norway in 1875, he first began visiting the Adirondacks in 1915 from New York City, where he worked. Jackrabbit was known for his skiing prowess and marathon ski tours. In 1919 he moved his business (he was a mechanical engineer selling heavy equipment) to Montreal and installed his family at the Lake Placid Club, visiting them on weekends. That winter he skied Marcy, Algonquin, and Whiteface. The following year, he teamed up with Langmuir and Apperson for an assault on the as-yet-unskied Haystack Mountain. Climbing from Upper Ausable Lake, Langmuir eventually turned back. Apperson and Jackrabbit continued on, arriving on the summit just as the sun set. Jackrabbit waxed poetic about that moment, as Alice Johannsen quotes him in her biography of her father, *The Legendary Jackrabbit Johannsen*:

We stood there together on the top of Haystack and looked over there towards the setting sun. The sky was a wonderful rose. To the northwest trailed the peaks of the Great Range, with Giant in the far distance. All the intervening peaks were basking in the sunset glow. High overhead rode the full moon, which we knew would give us plenty of light as we picked our way down again through the thick forest back to our Camp on the Upper Ausable.

Jackrabbit Johannsen in 1932. Photo courtesy Peggy Johannsen Austin collection.

It was a sight neither of us would ever forget, for that moment we saw the world below us as though it were frozen in time. There was no past, no future, just the present. And it was unspeakably beautiful!

Jackrabbit's most enduring contribution to the Adirondacks is the spirit of skiing that he exemplified. Jackrabbit found opportunities where others saw only obstacles. An English skier wrote of a 1922 outing with him: "Mr. Johannsen is a believer in his skis….When there is snow, he skis in that, but he has no unreasonable prejudices against rocks, stumps or roots, provided they are white in parts at least."

His daughter, Peggy Johannsen Austin, described his technique for me:

His pièce de résistance was what he called "bushwhacking." He could hop around like a rabbit, and that's why he got his name, "Jackrabbit." He always said, "Never stay on two skis at once. Always jump—keep moving your weight back and forth all the time so you're never stuck in a rut. That was his technique. He really did float and hop around trees.

Jackrabbit believed that long tours were the essence of the ski experience. That sensibility has continued among Adirondack skiers, who think nothing of a 15-mile round-trip tour up Mount Marcy, or of even longer excursions. Jackrabbit Johannsen died in 1987 at the age of 111. He skied until the age of 108, and is said to have attributed his longevity to his motto, "Ski ski ski!"

In 1932, the Winter Olympics were held in Lake Placid. The Winter Games featured cross-country skiing but no downhill events. It further catalyzed the growth and development of Nordic skiing in the region.

The Whiteface Ski Trail before lifts, 1938.
Photo courtesy Jim Goodwin Collection.

The 1930s was the era of down-mountain skiing in the Adirondacks. It was during this period that the Wright Peak Ski Trail was cut, and the Van Hoevenberg Trail up Mount Marcy was widened for skiing (for more on this history, see the chapters on the Wright Peak Ski Trail and Mount Marcy, respectively). In 1938 Lake Placid residents financed the cutting of the Whiteface Ski Trail on Little Whiteface Mountain. With a 2,700-foot vertical drop, this 2-mile-long down-mountain run became the first Class A race trail in the Adirondacks. The Whiteface trail was an anomaly: it was built on land owned by a timber company, so it could be cut wide and fast. The cutting of ski trails elsewhere in Adirondack Park was sharply limited by conservation restrictions, so skiing remained limited to a die-hard core of outdoorspeople.

Jim Goodwin, who began guiding trips in the Adirondacks in the 1920s and served in the famous ski troops of the U.S. Army Tenth Mountain Division, told me, "The tragedy was that because of the 'forever wild' laws, the Adirondacks had to lose out on having decent ski trails cut like the CCC was cutting in Vermont. So skiing in the Adirondacks really fell way behind."

The down-mountain era began to fade as small lift-serviced ski areas began popping up around the Adirondacks and in New England. Marble Mountain Ski Area opened near Lake Placid in 1948. It was replaced a decade later by the Whiteface Ski Area, the largest Adirondack ski resort to date. The venerable down-mountain Whiteface Trail was incorporated into the downhill ski area (the current

Wilderness Trail roughly follows its course). As happened all around New England, people quickly warmed to the idea of chairlifts and abandoned the old ski trails, leaving them to grow in.

SKI TO DIE

Development restrictions in the Adirondacks had an unintended effect: They spawned a "forever wild" style of skiing that was unique to the Adirondacks. Narrow trail skiing was elevated to a high art. Adirondack skiers began to strike out for the highest, wildest terrain on their cross-country skis. In so doing, they redefined the sense of what is possible on freeheel skis.

In the early 1970s, a small group of local rock climbers led by Geoff Smith of Plattsburgh started venturing into the High Peaks on skis. Dubbing themselves the American Eider Schussboomers, this wild-eyed group of mountaineers adapted their bold, exploratory mindset to backcountry skiing. They thought little of barreling down a narrow mountain trail on their skinny wooden cross-country racing skis, if only because they didn't know that most people dismissed such skiing as impossible. Inadvertently, they were becoming phenomenally good skiers.

As friendly competition grew among this clan of skiers, they adopted a new name. The Ski to Die Club captured the boldness, commitment, and sense of humor of the group. "A lot of the competitiveness of climbing—the camaraderie, the goading—carries over into skiing," insists Smith. Take, for example, the Ski to Die notion of "turnbacks."

"A turnback is when you ski something so horrific or frightening or so rotten that the guy you're with just looks at it, packs his backpack, turns around and leaves. There are many reasons not to ski something, but the idea of getting a turnback—that makes it even better," he says. Long before the term "extreme skiing" was coined, members of the Ski to Die Club were aiming their skinny skis down slides, streambeds, narrow trails, and virtually anywhere they could think of to slide.

The Ski to Die Club, whose elusive members still roam the highest peaks in search of the most elegant lines and best ski tours, captures the low glitz/high adventure soul of Adirondack skiing. Visitors to the Adirondacks will feel this infectious spirit on the ski trails described in this book.

As wild and innovative as their ski routes sound, the Ski to Diers insist that they're not doing anything new. Robbie Frenette, a veteran Ski to Dier who hails from an old family of Adirondack skiers, emphasizes that the Ski to Die Club is simply the modern torchbearer for an old tradition.

"There's a long history of skiing in the Adirondacks," he points out. "Jackrabbit Johannsen was skiing Mount Marcy and the other High Peaks way back in the 1920s." Indeed, some of Jackrabbit's wilder descents of remote Adirondack peaks went unrepeated until the Ski to Die Club took up his mantle in the seventies. Frenette insists, "We're just continuing what Jackrabbit started."

17

Jackrabbit Trail

THE TOUR

The McKenzie Pond Trail from Lake Placid to Saranac Lake showcases the Jackrabbit Trail, a 35-mile-long trail that connects the towns of Paul Smiths, Saranac Lake, Lake Placid, and Keene. This is a scenic tour that includes woods, ponds, and mountains, with a nice mix of uphill, flat, and downhill skiing.

LENGTH

5.5 miles (Whiteface Inn to McKenzie Pond Road)

ELEVATION

Start: 1,970 feet (Whiteface Inn Road)

Highest point: 2,600 feet (McKenzie Pass); 2,873 feet (Haystack Mountain)

Finish: 1,600 feet (McKenzie Pond Road)

Vertical drop: 1,000 feet (McKenzie Pass to McKenzie Pond Road)

MAPS

* *Jackrabbit Trail Cross-Country Skier's Map* is available free at many stores, or from the Adirondack Ski Touring Council (see below).
* *Trails of the Adirondack High Peaks Region* (ADK)
* *The Adirondacks: High Peaks Region* (Adirondack Maps)
* USGS Saranac Lake (1979)

DIFFICULTY

Moderate

FEE

There is no fee for skiing from Whiteface Inn Road to McKenzie Pond Road. If you start in Lake Placid, there is a fee for using the groomed trails of the Whiteface Club Nordic Center.

146

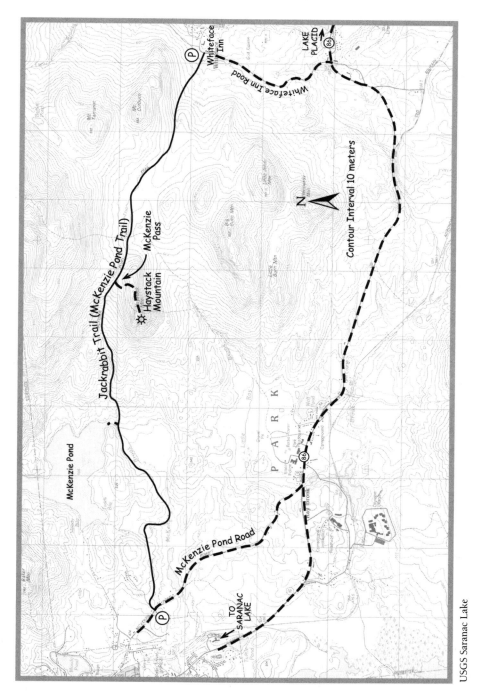

Whiteface
Inn

LAKE
PLACID

Whiteface Inn Road

Contour Interval 10 meters

N

McKenzie Pass

McKenzie Pond Trail

Jackrabbit Trail (McKenzie Pond Trail)

Haystack
Mountain

McKenzie Pond

P   A   R   K

McKenzie Pond Road

TO
SARANAC
LAKE

USGS Saranac Lake

JACKRABBIT TRAIL

HOW TO GET THERE

Driving west from Lake Placid on NY 86, turn right on Whiteface Inn Road (see signs for the inn). Go 1.3 miles, just past the entrance to the Whiteface Club. The Jackrabbit Trail starts on the left at phone pole 42.

To reach the McKenzie Pond Road trailhead (to spot a car or to start): From NY 86 just past Ray Brook, turn right on McKenzie Pond Road and drive 1.4 miles. A white sign for the Jackrabbit Trail is beside the road on the right.

ADDITIONAL INFORMATION

* For information about the Jackrabbit Trail, a free topographic map, and 24-hour trail conditions, contact the Adirondack Ski Touring Council: 518-523-1365.

In 1985 a small, dedicated group of skiing dreamers came up with a bold idea: they would create a long-distance town-to-town cross-country ski trail in the heart of the Adirondacks. The schemers, foremost among whom were Mark Ippolito, a local physician's assistant and avid skier, and Tony Goodwin, then the trail manager at the former Olympic cross-country skiing venue at Mount Van Hoevenberg, imagined a trail that would go from Tupper Lake to Keene. They drew their inspiration from Scandinavia and northern Europe, where skiing between towns is a time-honored pastime, and from Vermont, where the Catamount Trail was just getting established. They formed the Adirondack Ski Touring Council (ASTC) and named their scheme the Jackrabbit Trail, after the legendary Herman Smith "Jackrabbit" Johannsen (see the Mount Marcy chapter for more on Johannsen).

Tony Goodwin, who as the executive director of the ASTC has championed the trail (and who is author of the fine guidebook, *Classic Adirondack Ski Tours*), recounts that "the idea was not entirely original. A 1933 map of Lake Placid not only showed ski trails connecting Keene and Saranac Lake. It also made downtown Lake Placid the center of a vast network that would have qualified it as a 'cross-country ski center' long before that term was coined." Goodwin and Ippolito set about scouting a route and cajoling numerous local landowners to allow a trail through their lands. The pair was helped by the discovery of a provision in state law that said that landowners who permit recreation on their property have "no duty to keep those premises safe." As permissions began flowing in, there remained just one detail to attend to: creating the trail.

The daunting task of establishing some 35 miles of trails through the North Woods was made easier by the decision to use existing trails and logging roads wherever possible. Not that this let them off the hook: many old byways suffered from years, even decades, of neglect. Facing the task of restoring a particularly rough section of the Old Mountain Road in Keene (by then a badly eroded foot-path), the trailblazers turned to an unusual source of help. Trail-cutters were joined by inmates from the Moriah Shock Incarceration Facility in Mineville, a prison for first offenders who opt for six months of boot-camp-style work and schooling instead of a longer sentence. The resulting spectacle had guards, inmates, and Jackrabbit Trail volunteers all working side by side hefting 500-pound boulders, building bridges, and clearing brush. As a result of these efforts, Old Mountain Road is now well graded and skiable with only six inches of snow, instead of requiring two feet.

The Jackrabbit Trail is now a thriving reality. The trail includes ungroomed backcountry sections as well as groomed trails through local cross-country ski centers (note that skiing on cross-country center trails requires the purchase of a trail pass). Part of the charm of the Jackrabbit Trail is that it travels through the towns of Lake Placid, Keene, Paul Smiths, and Saranac Lake. You can ski the trail and be oh-so-civilized, stopping for a drink or a meal along the way. Or you can opt for the more ascetic pleasure of using the trail to head for the hills where no one will disturb you. The long-term goal is to extend the trail all the way from Paul Smiths to Tupper Lake, but this final leg is still in the planning stages.

Making telemark turns on top of Haystack Mountain, just off the Jackrabbit Trail.

One of the best backcountry sections of the Jackrabbit Trail is the leg from Lake Placid to Saranac Lake. This tour travels through wilderness lands and includes a great 1.5-mile moderate downhill on which to make turns. Most people ski the trail from Lake Placid, as this maximizes the downhill skiing. It is possible to start right in Lake Placid; this will involve paying a trail fee at the Whiteface Club Nordic Center, however, so most people opt to start at the backcountry trailhead just across the road from the Whiteface Inn.

The trailhead on Whiteface Inn Road is poorly signed (see directions above), but the broad logging-road-cum-trail into the woods should be obvious. About 100 feet in on the trail is a small gray sign that informs you: McKenzie Pond Rd. 5.5 miles, Saranac Lake 7 miles. You proceed up a gentle logging road, which may be partially melted due to poor drainage. In the 1930s, the Civilian Conservation Corps upgraded this path from a logging road to a fire trail. It was intended as a way to get firefighters into this remote area if needed. Thanks to their meticulous road-building efforts, this trail has survived the ravages of time. What may once have been a make-work project for a local CCC camp has been reincarnated as a great ski trail.

The trail continues uphill, rising slowly along the flanks of McKenzie Mountain, which lies to the north. A short spur departs left to Fallen Leaf Pond, a water source for the Whiteface Inn. The Jackrabbit Trail soon goes from private to state land, marked by an ASTC register. Red plastic Jackrabbit Trail blazes mark the way. Beyond the register, the trail levels out and you ski along a beautiful plateau. The trail is lined by tall birches, then spruces and firs, which frame the path and transform it into a stately corridor through the wilds. You soon pass a lean-to and then arrive at a trail junction. A sign says that it is 2.1 miles to the summit of Haystack Mountain. Haystack Mountain is a worthy destination, but there is a quicker way to get there. Continue on up the Jackrabbit Trail to where it levels out, and stop before heading downhill. This height-of-land is McKenzie Pass. If you choose not to spot a car at the other end of this tour, a good option is ski to this pass, then return to your starting point.

Haystack Mountain (one of eleven peaks in the Adirondacks named Haystack) lies uphill through the woods to the south. It is a twenty-minute detour to ski up through open woods to the summit, a ledge that is open to the south. This perch boasts jaw-drop views of the Adirondacks, extending from Giant Mountain to the Seward Range and including most of the High Peaks. This side trip and vista are a worthwhile bonus on this tour. The ski back down from the Haystack summit to McKenzie Pass is brushy (this detour is for the views, not the turns), but it only takes a few minutes to backtrack.

From McKenzie Pass, the trail begins a fun 1.5-mile downhill cruise. The trail is wide enough to make turns, but gentle enough that you can go straight without picking up too much speed. The descent ends at a trail junction where you can turn right for a short detour to McKenzie Pond. There are beautiful views across the pond, and even a bench where you can sit and take it all in or just take a rest. This section of the Jackrabbit Trail continues through an impressive pine forest, then crosses a ball field before arriving at McKenzie Pond Road.

A final flourish is to finish this as a "Mexican tour": continue another 2 miles into Saranac Lake and end right at the Casa del Sol Mexican restaurant. To do this, cross McKenzie Pond Road and continue on the Jackrabbit Trail, which follows an old snowmobile trail here. The trail eventually turns and proceeds on an old railroad bed. Just before crossing a 30-foot-long trestle, turn left and head into the town of Saranac Lake, where you will find this and other restaurants. Buen provecho!

OTHER OPTIONS

The Jackrabbit Trail can be divided up and skied as three other day trips, ranging from 6 to 9 miles. One of the prettier sections goes from Cascade Cross-Country Ski Center to Keene, ending with a 3-mile descent down the Old Mountain Road. Consult the Jackrabbit Trail map for details and directions to this and other tours.

18

Camp Peggy O'Brien Hut Tour

THE TOUR

The best hut-based ski tour in the Adirondacks. Glide into the heart of the High Peaks and lodge in the comfortable Camp Peggy O'Brien. There are numerous options for adventure skiing and snowboarding from the hut.

LENGTH

3.5 miles (the Garden parking area to Camp Peggy O'Brien)

ELEVATION

Start/finish: 1,523 feet (the Garden)
Highest point: 2,362 feet (Camp Peggy O'Brien)
Vertical drop: 839 feet

MAPS

 ❋ *Trails of the Adirondack High Peaks Region* (ADK)
 ❋ *The Adirondacks: High Peaks Region* (Adirondack Maps)
 ❋ USGS Keene Valley (1979)

DIFFICULTY

Moderate

FEE

Reservations to stay at Camp Peggy O'Brien should be made well in advance, since it is heavily booked. The hut holds twelve people, and you must book the entire hut; individual bed bookings are not accepted. Adirondack Mountain Club members receive a 10 percent discount. Reservations can be made up to fifty-one weeks in advance by calling the Adirondack Mountain Club at 518-523-3441. There is no telephone in the hut.

SNOWBOARDING

Camp Peggy O'Brien lies at the base of numerous mountains that offer excellent snowboarding. You will need snowshoes for the hike into the hut and up to the surrounding mountains.

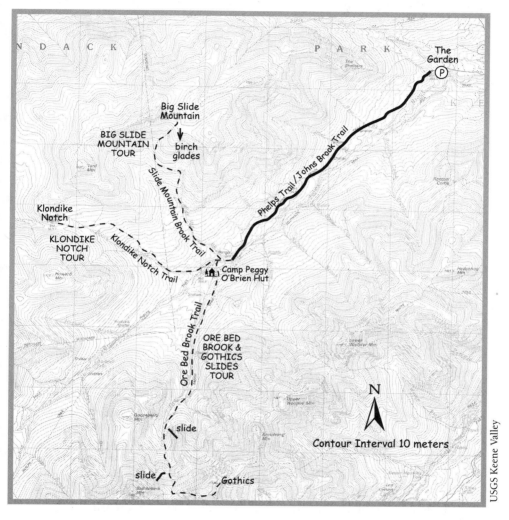

CAMP PEGGY O'BRIEN HUT TOUR

HOW TO GET THERE

From NY 73 in the center of Keene Valley, follow the Trail to the High Peaks sign and turn onto Interbrook Road. Follow this road, turning right across a bridge and then heading uphill. After 1.6 miles, the road ends in a large parking area known as the Garden. The trail to Johns Brook Lodge and Camp Peggy O'Brien departs from the west end of the parking lot.

ADDITIONAL INFORMATION

❋ Adirondack Mountain Club: 518-523-3441, www.adk.org

Something must be wrong. You are heading into the backcountry for a winter overnight, but you are strangely unencumbered. No ten-pound winter tent, no sack full of every shade of fleece and down, no provisions to lounge around at twenty below. In fact, you may be carrying a day pack.

Naturally, you assume this must be a description of the luxurious Tenth Mountain Trail in Colorado. Or a trip report from the Alps, Canadian Rockies, Tetons, or countless other famous ski ranges where huts and yurts abound. Think again: the Adirondacks are home to what is arguably the best hut-based skiing in the Northeast.

Western skiers and Europeans have been reveling in the comforts of winter huts for years. But easterners, for an odd variety of reasons, have been slow to catch on. One explanation is that eastern mountains are relatively accessible, diminishing the need for huts. Another reason may be that backcountry suffering has been a bit too honored a tradition in the Northeast, where the Puritan work ethic still holds sway.

In an impassioned essay entitled "A Plea for Huts," which appeared in the 1942 *American Ski Annual*, James Laughlin wrote:

> We must have huts in America for high mountain touring. Not just occasional isolated huts here and there, but groups of two and three (and later more) related huts in our principal mountain areas. Until we have them, the run of American skiers will never know what it means to tour, and, as anyone knows who has toured abroad, touring is the real cream of skiing....The ultimate in ski pleasure is to get off into the "big stuff," a high range far away from the world below, a world to itself of sun and snow, where, likely enough, the only tracks you will see will be those you make yourself....
>
> So here's to our chain of American huts! Soon may they come!

It was not soon enough. It took until the mid-1980s, when the Tenth Mountain Trail in Colorado was established, for American skiers to truly understand the pleasures of which Laughlin wrote. The beautiful log cabins sprinkled around the high mountains of Colorado and linked by ski trails have been a smashing success. Skiers who travel the Tenth Mountain Trail return as converts to the cause of going light and staying in style in the wilderness.

The two best-known winter huts in the Northeast are located in the White Mountains of New Hampshire and are run by the Appalachian Mountain Club. The AMC huts are relatively rugged affairs with unheated sleeping quarters. They essentially offer indoor winter camping. They are nice, but basic.

Into this vacuum, enter the Peggy O'Brien Hut—or "Camp Peggy O'Brien," as it is officially called. The hut was built by the Adirondack Mountain Club (ADK) in 1989 and opened for business in early 1990. The hut was named for Peggy O'Brien, a former vice president of the Adirondack Mountain Club who was chair of the Johns Brook Lodge (JBL) Committee for eleven years. She was nicknamed "Mrs. JBL" for her efforts to promote the forest lodge.

Camp Peggy O'Brien is situated in the heart of the High Peaks, the tallest mountains in New York State. Surrounded by the ice-plastered face of Gothics, long snow-filled streambeds, and the skiable summit domes of Mount Haystack and Mount Marcy, this hut showcases first-class backcountry ski terrain. It also redefines the standards of comfort in eastern backcountry huts.

The 3.5-mile trail into Camp Peggy O'Brien meanders through a classic northern hardwood forest. Originally plied by loggers at the turn of the century, this route led to what was once a bustling lumber camp that was the base of operations for logging the surrounding peaks. The axmen took timber from as high as 3,800 feet on nearby Big Slide Mountain, hauling huge loads out by horse team. After the loggers left, they were replaced by a hermit named Mel Hathaway, who occupied the abandoned logging camp until 1926. The logging camp has since been replaced by a ranger cabin and Johns Brook Lodge, a bustling Adirondack Mountain Club hut that sleeps twenty-eight and is open May through October.

From the Garden, the yellow-blazed trail known as the Phelps Trail or the Johns Brook Trail, climbs moderately. At 0.5 mile, come to a junction with the South-side Trail, an alternate but equidistant route to JBL. The Phelps Trail continues to climb gently, with plenty of small turns and twists, and a number of brook crossings. The route finally passes a campsite, then makes a hard left and drops down to a ranger outpost. Turn right, pass the junction with the Slide Mountain Brook Trail, then turn left to cross an airy, open-sided bridge over Johns Brook. Thread through a dark stand of conifers, and you soon arrive at your evening destination. The discreetly located Camp Peggy O'Brien stays hidden until you are practically on its front porch. There, nestled among the fir trees is a handsome wood home with a steeply pitched green roof, blond wood porch, and a handmade ski rack. Here is a backcountry lodge that Scandinavian and even Colorado hut enthusiasts would admire.

Inside the hut you are greeted not by a cold fireplace and a stack of wood waiting to be chopped and lit, but by a switch. This miraculous invention controls

Skiers taking a snow day at the Camp Peggy O'Brien Hut.

the propane stove, heater, and lights. It is a novelty indeed to encounter such easy living in the heart of a winter wilderness. The post-and-beam hut features high vaulted ceilings and giant beams, and is lined in beautiful knotty-pine boards. The camp is also equipped with a full set of cooking and eating utensils. Sleeping is on bunk beds with mattresses. Besides your usual day pack of clothing and equipment for backcountry skiing, bring a lightweight sleeping bag and food. These amenities are your cue to pack light. That's part of the pleasure of a hut tour.

There are numerous skiing and snowboarding options from the hut. Here are some of the best:

BIG SLIDE MOUNTAIN

DIFFICULTY
Moderate/more difficult

One of the closest playgrounds to the hut is the extensive birch glade on nearby Big Slide Mountain. Backtracking across the bridge to the Slide Mountain Brook Trail, head uphill, and take note of the forest on the right side. Follow the trail for about a mile, crossing Slide Mountain Brook several times. The forest slowly transforms into a vast birch glade. Birches are a special treat for eastern skiers. They are typically found at around 3,000 feet and higher, where the snow lies lighter and deeper. Birches, like skiers, favor generous spacing, which makes them signposts luring you to some of the best turns on the mountain. There is also the unique aesthetic of the brilliant white bark, which radiates a warm yellow-gold as the sun drops in the late afternoon. The glades on Big Slide are particularly enticing: there is almost no undergrowth to bash through, just leisurely turns to carve as you please.

You have two choices for skiing. If you prefer a low-angle glade, simply leave the trail and head up into this birch glade, climbing as high as you like. The descent is on a moderate slope, where even novice skiers will enjoy banking turns through nature's gates. If you are looking for steeper terrain, continue uphill on the hiking trail until the junction with the trail to the Brothers at 2.1 miles. From here, you can drop downhill into the forest, which opens steadily into the vast birch glade that you saw from below.

GOTHICS SLIDES AND ORE BED BROOK

DIFFICULTY
Most difficult

For expert Adirondack skiers, the ultimate descents are on the steep slides that lie throughout the range, and in the streambeds that form natural passageways through the mountains. The slides are typically difficult to reach and often involve technical mountaineering challenges. These classic ski mountaineering routes require intimate knowledge of the terrain.

Gothics offers skiers and snowboarders the opportunity to ski two nontechnical lower-angle slides and a streambed, all of which are easily accessible from Camp

Peggy O'Brien. Gothics is a majestic mountain, with a triple summit and huge ice-plastered rock faces. The summit gets its name because its appearance "suggested Gothic architecture," recounts the ADK *Guide to Adirondack Trails: High Peaks*.

From the hut, ski up the Woodsfall Trail and turn right at the junction with the Ore Bed Brook Trail. The trail climbs steadily, and at 2.3 miles it crosses a large slide. This 500-foot slide offers beautiful views of Saddleback Mountain, the rock cliffs on Gooseberry Mountain, and the sweeping face of Gothics. You can ski or snowboard this lower-angle slide, and then continue down by skiing in Ore Bed Brook. The brook is a spacious corridor in which you can enjoy skirting the natural rollovers and drops that characterize a small mountain waterway.

There is also the option to continue farther up the Ore Bed Brook Trail until you reach a second, longer—and somewhat steeper—slide that runs parallel to the trail. You can ski this slide, which also empties into the wide-open Ore Bed Brook drainage. The brook and the trail both lead back to Camp Peggy O'Brien.

This is a tantalizing and enjoyable introduction to Adirondack slide skiing. Gothics also has steeper and more committing slides, not described here, that involve technical ski mountaineering. If you are an expert skier who is new to the Adirondacks, consider hiring a guide if you want to explore the steepest, wildest side of these mountains.

Note that on any open slope of 30 degrees or greater in steepness, *you must assess the avalanche hazard before venturing onto it, and back off if conditions are unstable.* Avalanche hazard is a very real threat on the exposed Adirondack slides. In February 2000, one skier was killed and another seriously injured when they were caught in an avalanche while skiing the large slide on the east face of Wright Peak.

For more on avalanches, see the chapter "Mountaineering Skills and Avalanches."

KLONDIKE NOTCH

DIFFICULTY
Moderate

This is a moderate ski tour to a scenic pass. The red-blazed Klondike Notch Trail departs from JBL and follows a trail up the left bank of Black Brook. At 1.3 miles it passes a junction with the trail to Big Slide Mountain. You reach Klondike Notch, a saddle between Howard and Yard mountains, at 1.7 miles. This is an 866-foot climb from JBL. From the notch, you can ski back to the hut or continue skiing to Adirondack Loj, which is 7.3 miles from JBL. The ski back to JBL from Klondike Notch is pure pleasure, skiing either on the trail or through the trees.

19

Wright Peak Ski Trail

THE TOUR
A ski tour on Wright Peak in the Adirondack High Peaks, offering panoramic views from the summit and an exciting descent of the historic Wright Peak Ski Trail.

LENGTH
1 mile (Wright Peak Ski Trail); 7 miles round-trip (Adirondack Loj to Wright Peak summit)

ELEVATION
Start/finish: 2,179 feet (Adirondack Loj); 3,100 feet (bottom of Wright Peak Ski Trail)

Highest point: 4,580 feet (Wright Peak summit)

Vertical drop: 2,401 feet (total tour); 1,480 feet (Wright Peak Ski Trail)

MAPS
* *Trails of the Adirondack High Peaks Region* (ADK)
* *The Adirondacks: High Peaks Region* (Adirondack Maps)
* USGS Keene Valley (1979)

Note: These maps all show Wright Peak and its hiking trail, but none show the Wright Peak Ski Trail.

DIFFICULTY
More difficult

FEE
A parking fee is required at the High Peaks Information Center parking lot.

SNOWBOARDING
The descent of Wright Peak and its ski trail is a fine backcountry snowboard tour. Snowshoes will be needed for the ascent, and it is necessary to walk on the rolling Van Hoevenberg Trail.

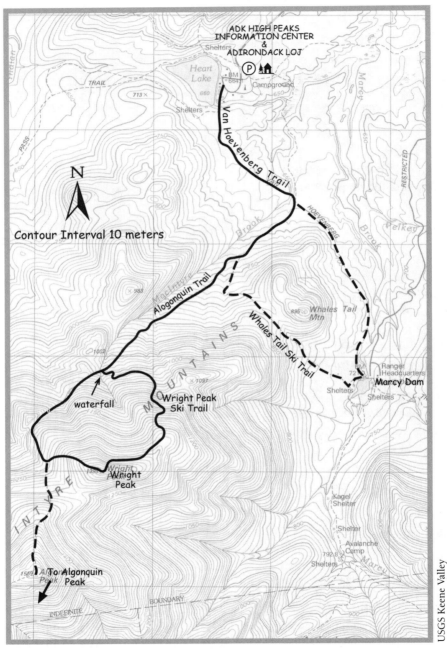

WRIGHT PEAK SKI TRAIL

HOW TO GET THERE

From Lake Placid, drive east on NY 73 about 3 miles. Turn right (south) on the Adirondack Loj Road and proceed approximately 5 miles to the end of the road. Park at the High Peaks Information Center. Maps and supplies are available from the information center, which is open daily from 8:00 A.M. to 5:00 P.M.

ADDITIONAL INFORMATION

✳ Adirondack Loj: 518-523-3441, www.adk.org

Wright Peak lies in the heart of the Adirondack High Peaks. The ski tour to its scenic open summit and the descent of the historic Wright Peak Ski Trail is an Adirondack classic. It offers all the best elements of a great tour: an enjoyable climb, panoramic summit views, and a ski trail roomy enough to make many turns on. Wright Peak is the northernmost summit of the 8-mile-long MacIntyre Range, whose most prominent summit is Algonquin Peak, the second highest mountain in New York. Wright Peak was named after New York Governor Silas Wright.

The Wright Peak Ski Trail is a byproduct of the unique and peculiar politics of the Adirondack Park. In 1892, the New York state legislature created the Adirondack State Park, which included all private land within park boundaries, and the Adirondack Forest Preserve. Two years later, New York State citizens voted to include into the state constitution a provision stating that the 2.5 million-acre Forest Preserve would remain "forever wild." The "forever wild" clause was interpreted to mean that no trail exceeding 10 feet in width could be cut.

Enter the late Hal Burton. An avid skier and newspaperman, and later a veteran of the U.S. Army Tenth Mountain Division, Burton was eager to have a good down-mountain ski run someplace within the Adirondacks. He and his friends watched enviously as the CCC was building exciting ski trails throughout New England, while Adirondack skiers were forced to negotiate narrow, unforgiving hiking trails. Burton decided that Wright Peak would make an excellent location for a ski trail. It was easily accessible and had a good gradient for skiing. Burton managed to persuade state conservation commissioner Lithgow Osborne that he could build a "self-concealing" trail, and Osborne defended the concept at numerous public hearings. At one public meeting, a conservationist sniped at Osborne, "I gather you propose to approve this trail. When will construction begin?"

"The rangers," Osborne replied, "are already halfway up the mountain."

That was almost as far as the Wright Peak Ski Trail got. In October 1938, forest fires swept through the Catskills, and all available rangers from the Adirondacks were transferred south to fight the fires. The rangers had just begun cutting the Wright Peak Ski Trail when they were forced to abandon the project. But Hal Burton was determined. He recounted later in the *Lake Placid News*, "I happened to have saved $400 for the down payment on a new car. Believe it or not, cars were cheap in those days, and so was the pay for woodcutters. The $400 went for the hire of guides from the Ausable Club. The new car had to wait a year, but the trail was completed."

The Wright Peak Ski Trail opened for skiing in December 1938. The trail was designed by legendary Dartmouth ski coach Otto Schneibs and New York State ski trail designer Bob St. Louis (who was later killed in World War II). Schneibs wanted wide trails for speed, but St. Louis scaled it down. They followed old logging roads most of the way. Burton skied the run and was satisfied that his investment had paid off. He wrote: "What a trail! Fairly narrow, to be sure, but it is still one of the most beautiful down-mountain runs in the East—frosted with rime on the upper reaches, brightened by sun on the lower, with the best and most reliable snow in the Lake Placid area."

The Wright Peak Ski Trail was nearly done in by its many admirers. Within a few years, Burton skied the trail and "found only congestion—one skier every five minutes." He declared to the director of lands and forests, "This is intolerable." He proposed alleviating the backcountry traffic jam by building a new ski area in the Adirondacks. The seeds were thus sown for the creation of Whiteface Ski Area. Little could Burton have imagined in the 1930s that Whiteface and its lift-serviced ilk would nearly drive the Wright Peak Ski Trail to extinction. The Wright Peak Ski Trail was maintained until about the early 1960s, after which the trail faded into obscurity.

With the resurgence of backcountry skiing in the 1980s, Adirondack skiers were eagerly exploring any new terrain that held the potential for good skiing. Like the previous generation, young Adirondack skiers chafed under the restrictions of the "forever wild" rule. Then Mark Ippolito, a local physician's assistant with seemingly boundless energy for ski-related projects (see the Jackrabbit Trail chapter for another of his endeavors), did some research and discovered the existence of the Wright Peak Ski Trail on old maps. Since state law allowed for old trails to be restored, Ippolito got permission from park officials to take a crew of volunteers and cut their way up what they believed was the Wright Peak Ski Trail in the spring of 1987. Tony Goodwin, the executive director of the Adirondack Ski Touring Council, finished the job in 1989. But no sooner had the saws stopped than an outcry ensued. Angry conservationists insisted that the "new old trail" was wider than 10 feet and that it did not follow the old route. As proof, they noted that some of the trees that had been cut were older than the original trail! The trailblazers diplomatically assured the critics that a few large trees had to be removed for safety reasons, and the controversy died down.

The born-again Wright Peak Ski Trail was never recut all the way to the summit out of concern that summer hikers would start using the trail and trample fragile alpine vegetation. As a result, the top of the trail remains intentionally obscure. That has succeeded in warding off the hikers, but it has also stymied many a skier hoping to drop into the trail from the top. I will offer directions here, but if you

Gliding down the bottom of the Wright Peak Ski Trail.

want to be certain you find the trail, your best bet is to climb it from the bottom, where it crosses the main hiking trail.

From the High Peaks Information Center (HPIC), take the Van Hoevenberg Trail 0.9 mile until reaching a junction with the trail to Algonquin and Wright Peak. While on the Van Hoevenberg Trail, you will see several skier bypasses that cross the main hiking trail; just ski on whichever path is in better condition, since they all go to the same place. From the Algonquin Trail junction, proceed straight ahead and follow the yellow-blazed trail to Algonquin and Wright Peak. You soon cross a junction with the Whale's Tale Ski Trail, which was cut in 1937 and leads up and over a saddle, then down to Marcy Dam. The Whale's Tale Ski Trail is now badly eroded and faces south, so it needs at least a foot of snow to be skiable.

The trail toward Wright Peak and Algonquin starts gradually uphill, then crosses a brook at around 3,000 feet and pitches up more steeply. The trail soon ascends through a stunning grove of birch trees. The green forest recedes, and you enter a world of white on white. The bottom of the Wright Peak Ski Trail intersects the hiking trail at 3,100 feet (there is a trail sign). Either climb up the ski trail from here, or continue upward on the main hiking trail, soon crossing an old abandoned trail at an arrow. A few hundred yards further is a camping area, and then a prominent waterfall that crosses the trail and empties into a major drainage.

After 3.1 miles you reach a junction; the yellow-blazed trail continues to Algonquin Peak in 0.8 mile, and the blue-blazed trail leads to the summit of Wright Peak in 0.4 mile. As you climb steeply toward the Wright Peak summit, you soon reach timberline. It is best to suit up for the summit just before stepping out onto the rocky ridge. You will have to remove skis and climb over the rocks to the actual summit. Be warned that the summit can be plastered in rime ice and footing can be treacherous. Expect the full force of the weather on the exposed summit, and don't attempt it if visibility is poor or conditions are deteriorating.

From the summit of Wright Peak there are fantastic views of the enormous slides on Mount Colden, the snow-plastered dome of Algonquin Peak, and Mount Marcy. The 360-degree panorama continues with a view of Whiteface and Heart Lake to the north.

After savoring this incredible mountainscape, it is time to find the top of the Wright Peak Ski Trail. From the summit, walk along the rocky ridge about 50 feet directly toward Mount Marcy. Then stop and look down toward Heart Lake. You will see a prominent rock about 100 feet down with a geologically rare right-angle corner on it. The rock points directly at Heart Lake (that's the lake to the north in the shape of—you guessed it—a heart). It's as if Heart Lake and the rock are pointing at each other. Walk down off the summit ridge to this rock. Just above the rock, turn right, scramble over a small ridge, and see a narrow chute that heads downhill. Ski this chute about 80 feet until it ends, then look for where a 6- to 8-foot-wide trail breaks right. Follow this trail as it contours west (toward Marcy), then begins gently descending. The trail opens gradually and maintains a double fall line. It repeatedly traverses, then drops. The trail progressively widens to about 15 feet and the skiing becomes steadily better. The Wright Peak Ski Trail then drops into the huge birch glade that you saw from the hiking trail. This is a highlight, as the fall-line shots get longer through this gorgeous forest. The ski trail snaps back on itself several times, like a snake scrambling downhill.

After about a mile, you reach the hiking trail you climbed up on. As you continue down swinging turns on the wide hiking trail, you may have the sense that you are still on the ski trail. That's because you are: The original Wright Peak Ski Trail continued all the way to the junction with the Whale's Tale Ski Trail. In 1974, the Algonquin Trail was relocated to this lower section of the Wright Peak Ski Trail. The result is that there is plenty of room to swing turns on the spacious footpath. Beware of several stream crossings as you head lower. Continue to retrace your route back to the Van Hoevenberg Trail and the HPIC parking area.

The Wright Peak Ski Trail captures the spirit of the best 1930s-era trails. It rolls with the terrain, twisting and turning all the way down. You are truly skiing the nuances of this mountain, and there is never a predictable moment. The hiking trail offers a rousing but reasonable finish to the ski trail. You do not need to be an expert skier for this route—a good snowplow and the ability to stop when needed will see you through. The highlights are the dramatic alpine terrain and vistas on the summit, and the powder you enjoy all the way down.

20

Avalanche Pass

THE TOUR

A ski tour from Adirondack Loj over Avalanche Pass to the high alpine Avalanche Lake and Lake Colden. The tour features unrivaled scenery and fun downhill skiing.

LENGTH

12 miles round-trip

ELEVATION

Start/finish: 2,179 feet (High Peaks Information Center)
Highest point: 3,100 feet (Avalanche Pass)
Vertical drop: 921 feet

MAPS

* *Trails of the Adirondack High Peaks Region* (ADK)
* *The Adirondacks: High Peaks Region* (Adirondack Maps)
* USGS Keene Valley (1979) and USGS Mount Marcy (1979)

DIFFICULTY

More difficult

FEE

A parking fee is required at the ADK High Peaks Information Center parking lot.

SNOWBOARDING

The descent from Avalanche Pass on the ski trail is a fun, moderate backcountry snowboard route. Snowshoes will be needed for the ascent on the hiking trail, and it will be necessary to walk out from Marcy Dam.

HOW TO GET THERE

From Lake Placid, drive east on NY 73 about 3 miles. Turn south on Adirondack Loj Road and proceed approximately 5 miles to the end of the road. Park at the High Peaks Information Center. Maps and supplies are available from the information center, or see directions below to Marcy Dam Truck Trail.

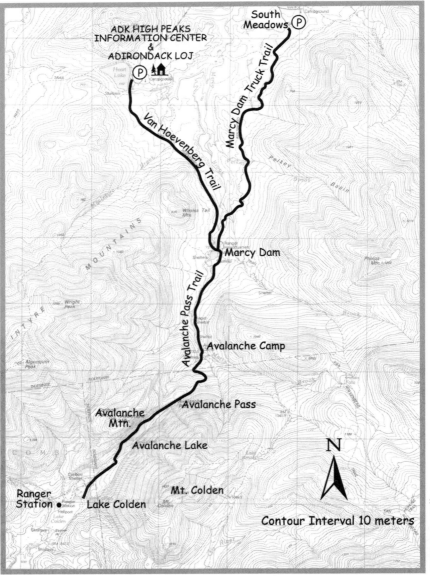

ADK HIGH PEAKS
INFORMATION CENTER
&
ADIRONDACK LOJ

South
Meadows Ⓟ

Ⓟ 🏠

Marcy Dam Truck Trail

Van Hoevenberg Trail

Marcy Dam

Avalanche Pass Trail

Avalanche Camp

Avalanche Pass

Avalanche
Mtn.

Avalanche Lake

Ranger
Station ●

Lake Colden

Mt. Colden

N

Contour Interval 10 meters

USGS Keene Valley
USGS Mount Marcy

AVALANCHE PASS

ADDITIONAL INFORMATION
✳ Adirondack Loj: 518-523-3441, www.adk.org

Skiing over Avalanche Pass to Lake Colden is one of the most spectacular ski tours in the eastern U.S. This tour offers the combination of a climb and descent on a historic ski trail and, most of all, a trip through a landscape of incredible grandeur. The highlight of the tour is skiing across Avalanche Lake, a narrow half-mile-long passageway hemmed in by cliffs that rise directly out of the frozen waterway.

The ski tour into Avalanche Pass has long been a favorite among winter visitors to the Adirondacks. Jim Goodwin, a former Adirondack guide who began hiking and skiing in the High Peaks in the 1920s, recalls that by 1930 the ski in to Avalanche Pass "was very popular and just as beautiful as it is today. I skied that a number of times in those days, and I never remember a time when the track wasn't broken." He recalls that the trail "was fairly rugged. Intermediate skiers could handle it all right. Usually they'd fall one or two times." The 1939 Federal Writers' Project guidebook *Skiing in the East* described the tour as "a fine trip for intermediate skiers."

The ski tour into Avalanche Pass goes through Marcy Dam, the busy backcountry crossroads of the High Peaks. There are two routes into Marcy Dam: The most direct route (2.1 miles) is to take the Van Hoevenberg Trail from the ADK High Peaks Information Center (next to Adirondack Loj) to Marcy Dam. This trail is heavily used by hikers, snowshoers, and climbers, and is often icy. The better ski route follows the Marcy Dam Truck Trail from South Meadows. It is slightly longer (2.8 miles), but this graded truck trail can be skied with just a couple of inches of snow, and the broad path is a fast ski. To reach the trailhead in South Meadows, take the Adirondack Loj Road and turn left at 3.7 miles at the sign for South Meadows. Drive 1 mile to a parking area. The truck trail leaves from here. There is presently no fee to park at South Meadows.

Views of the peaks get better as you continue the gradual 265-foot climb on the truck trail. Once at Marcy Dam, you are forced to a halt by the vista in front of you. To the west lies Wright Peak. You peer directly at the two prominent landslides on the east face of Wright Peak, which occurred during Hurricane Floyd in the fall of 1999. The broad slide on the left was the scene of a tragic avalanche accident in February 2000 in which one skier was killed and another was badly injured. You also have views here of Avalanche Pass, the height-of-land between Mount Colden and Avalanche Mountain. It is 2.2 miles to Avalanche Pass from here.

From the trail register at Marcy Dam, follow the trail to Mount Marcy, passing lean-tos (which can be used for camping). After about 100 yards, the trail to Avalanche Pass diverges to the right and is marked with yellow plastic disks.

The trail is flat at first, then rises gently for 1.1 miles, reaching the Avalanche Lean-to. From the lean-to, the hiking and ski trails diverge. Skiers should follow the ski trail—it is less rocky and icy, and you get to preview what you will ski down. Snowboarders and snowshoers must stay on the hiking trail. The next stretch to Avalanche Lake is unfairly dubbed "misery mile." While it certainly climbs steadily, the angle is quite reasonable, and climbing skins are not needed. The ski trail crisscrosses the hiking trail a number of times. If you decide to walk rather than ski, please take the hiking trail, which is often firmly packed. Post-holing the ski trail will ruin the ski experience for others.

There can be no mistaking where you are when you reach Avalanche Pass. The pass now lives up to its name: In the fall of 1999, Hurricane Floyd lashed the Adirondacks with high winds and heavy rain. The result was a massive landslide that swept down the slopes above and buried Avalanche Pass in 50 feet of debris. It took rangers days to hack through the tangle of trees and boulders that had piled up on the pass in order to reopen the trail. Peering up from the pass, there is now a 1,000-foot-long and several-hundred-foot-wide rock slide ripped into the mountain. Avalanche Pass offers a graphic display of how active the Adirondack environment is, as landslides and even earthquakes occur here with some regularity. Seeing the massive trees picked up and tossed down the moun-

Skiing across windswept Avalanche Lake beneath the cliffs of Mount Colden.

tain like Lincoln Logs leaves you with a renewed respect for the awesome forces of nature.

The short descent from Avalanche Pass to Avalanche Lake offers a quick introduction to classic Adirondack trail skiing. It swoops downhill, then breezes around wide turns, and finally deposits you abruptly onto Avalanche Lake.

Avalanche Lake is a place where nature's drama is acted out in bold strokes. The view from the frozen windswept lake is of an utterly wild landscape. Black rock walls of Mount Colden and Avalanche Mountain soar up on both sides of you, dwarfing all who pass here. Mount Colden is raked with slides, and curtains of ice pour down onto the lake. Wind funnels through here, forcing you to move along briskly and protect yourself. This is a landscape unlike any other in the region for its accessibility and drama. It is a magnificent natural gallery that leaves you awestruck.

Ski straight across the lake to its southwest end. At 0.3 mile from the lake, you come to a trail junction. The sign indicates that the trail to Algonquin and Lake Colden goes to the right. Ignore the sign and simply ski straight ahead on flat ground, following an old phone line. You emerge onto Lake Colden in a few minutes.

From Lake Colden there are spectacular views of all the slides on Mount Colden. You also have sweeping views of the interior mountains, including a beautiful vantage point from which to view Algonquin Peak and the Bear Claw Slide on its south face. There is a ranger outpost at Lake Colden which is staffed in winter.

Returning to Avalanche Pass, you are ready to begin a classic Adirondack ski descent. From the top of the pass, the trail tumbles downhill like a roller coaster, complete with swooping downhills, banked turns, and forgiving run outs where you need them. Be careful to remain on the ski trail, which is cut wide for skiing, and not the hiking trail, which is rutted and narrow. The ski trail has many long, flat sections where you can slow down. That is the beauty of this descent: it never gets too pushy, and a well-placed snowplow should suffice to check your speed. This is eastern trail skiing at its best. You turn where the trail turns, and cruise where it relaxes. The skiing is fun and fast, but the intensity level on this trail is several notches below the Mount Marcy descent, which is more relentless. Consider the Avalanche Pass descent your bachelor's degree in eastern trail skiing. It is great preparation for the master class that awaits you on Mount Marcy.

Passing the Avalanche Lean-to, it is still a steady downhill cruise all the way to Marcy Dam. You might consider camping at one of the Marcy Dam lean-tos. This would allow you to ski Avalanche Pass one day, camp in the heart of the High Peaks, and finish by skiing Mount Marcy the next day. This Adirondack "grand slam" will give you a full appreciation of what this great range has to offer. And it will undoubtedly keep you coming back for more.

21
Mount Marcy

THE TOUR

The ski tour from Adirondack Loj to Mount Marcy, New York's highest peak, is one of the great ski mountaineering adventures in the East. It features panoramic views and legendary trail skiing.

LENGTH

14.8 miles round-trip

ELEVATION

Start/finish: 2,179 feet (High Peaks Information Center)
Highest point: 5,344 feet (Mount Marcy summit)
Vertical drop: 3,165 feet

MAPS

* *Trails of the Adirondack High Peaks Region* (ADK)
* *The Adirondacks: High Peaks Region* (Adirondack Maps)
* USGS Keene Valley (1979)

DIFFICULTY

Most difficult

FEE

There is a fee to park at the ADK High Peaks Information Center.

SNOWBOARDING

A highlight of the Mount Marcy tour is the epic 5-mile downhill ride from the summit to Marcy Dam. You will have to hike or snowshoe the rolling 2 miles from Marcy Dam back to your car.

HOW TO GET THERE

From Lake Placid, drive east on NY 73 about 3 miles. Turn right (south) on the Adirondack Loj Road and proceed 5 miles to the end of the road. Park at the High Peaks Information Center. Maps and supplies are available at the information center, which is open daily from 8:00 A.M. to 5:00 P.M.

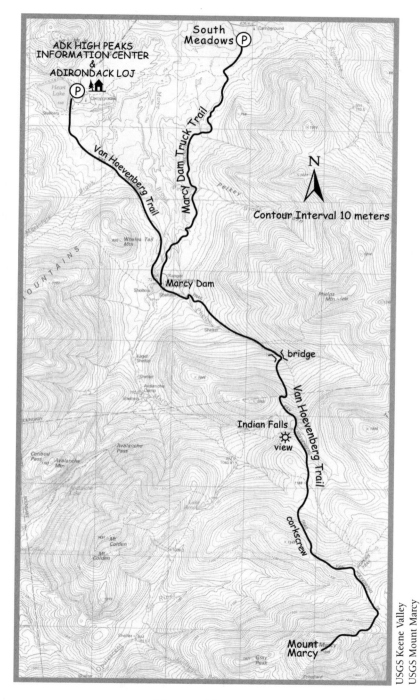

South
Meadows Ⓟ

ADK HIGH PEAKS
INFORMATION CENTER
&
ADIRONDACK LOJ

Ⓟ

Van Hoevenberg Trail

Marcy Dam Truck Trail

N

Contour Interval 10 meters

Marcy Dam

bridge

Van Hoevenberg Trail

Indian Falls
☼
view

corkscrew

Mount
Marcy

USGS Keene Valley
USGS Mount Marcy

MOUNT MARCY

ADDITIONAL INFORMATION

✳ Adirondack Loj: 518-523-3441, www.adk.org

If you are looking for the best trail skiing in North America, look no further than Mount Marcy. The highest peak in New York State, the dome-capped, 5,344-foot Mount Marcy has lured backcountry skiers for a century.

The main attractions on Mount Marcy are the sweeping summit views and the 7.4-mile, 3,100-vertical-foot, turn-packed descent. This is eastern trail skiing at its finest. You follow the serpentine Von Hoevenberg Trail as it snakes, jogs, drops, and rolls down the mountain. The trail has a personality and a sense of humor, constantly surprising you around each bend. Ski Mount Marcy once and you will be addicted to the thrill.

Mount Marcy has had a singular pull on mountaineers and skiers over the past two centuries. The mountain was first climbed on August 5, 1837, by a party led by Ebenezer Emmons, a chemistry professor at Williams College who headed a section of the Geological Survey of New York. Emmons named the peak in honor of Governor William Learned Marcy. The mountain also bears the Indian name Tahawus, which means "cloud splitter," although the ADK's *Guide to Adirondack Trails* insists that local Indians did not actually use this name.

The first ski descent of Mount Marcy was made by John S. Apperson, Jean Canivet, and a third man in 1911. There are some claims of a ski ascent of Marcy by Apperson or Irving Langmuir as early as 1908, but these are dubious. Apperson worked for General Electric in Schenectady, New York. He is responsible for several other notable first descents in the Adirondacks, which he explored for much of his life (see the chapter "The Adirondacks: A Ski History").

While Apperson is credited with the first ski descent of Marcy, the most influential skier to set foot on Mount Marcy and its environs was unquestionably Herman Smith "Jackrabbit" Johannsen. Born in Norway in 1875, he first arrived in the Adirondacks in 1915. He settled in at the Lake Placid Club, where he frequently guided winter trips into the mountains. He was famous for undertaking huge ski tours. A typical Jackrabbit tour included skiing 9 miles from Lake Placid to Adirondack Loj, then continuing for another 7 miles to the Mount Marcy summit, and finally camping out in the mountains and continuing the next day. Following the 1932 Winter Olympics in Lake Placid, Jackrabbit took advantage of having the world's best skiers around by leading a group of them on one of his "pleasure tours": he went from Adirondack Loj to Indian Pass, down to Tahawus, and back to Lake Colden—an itinerary that hikers will take up to four days to cover. At Lake Colden, the fifty-six-year-old tour guide then asked whether his guests would like to bag Mount Marcy too. When none of the hardy men declined, he started up the 2,600-foot ascent. They skied back to the Loj by moonlight.

The trails up Mount Marcy were crude in the early days, and winter ascents were expeditions. On one trip, Jackrabbit brought a group of five men from Schenectady, New York, to ski into Avalanche Pass. After spending the night, the men fought their way up the snow-choked Opalescent and Feldspar Brooks to reach Lake Tear of the Clouds. Jackrabbit's daughter Alice captured the spirit of those early Marcy journeys in her wonderful biography, *The Legendary Jackrabbit Johannsen*: "A thousand feet above them loomed the bold top of Marcy, snow covered and trackless....When they finally set out again, it was with the sensation that they were real explorers, as they zigzagged their way out above the timber line, between patches of ice and snow, to the very top."

Skiing on Marcy improved slowly. In the late summer of 1935, a group of Adirondack skiers hiked up the Van Hoevenberg Trail in the rain and marked 127 trees for removal. Strict conservation rules forbade the widening of Adirondack trails. But the skiers pressed their case. "Cutting these trees would go far toward preventing broken bones among the skiers who were then fast multiplying," reported *The Ski Bulletin*. "Conservationists raised hell," recalled the late ski pioneer Hal Burton, who was on the scouting trip. But the skiers prevailed, and the trail was widened. At last, Adirondack skiers had a feasible ski route to the summit of Mount Marcy.

This made skiing on Mount Marcy possible, but not easy. In January 1937, *The Ski Bulletin* reported, "The Van Hoevenberg trail up Mount Marcy from Heart Lake is not a good downhill ski trail... .It is, however, a very good trail to ski." The writer, one P. F. Loope from the *Schenectady Gazette*, offered sage advice that still applies today: "At all places it is necessary to hold to a speed at which the skier can stop on short notice, for unless one knows every inch of the trail, a spill at high speed may mean plunging into a stump or stone buried under light snow." He concluded of the ski tour, "For one interested in rugged winter mountain scenery this trip is among the best available."

The ski tour up Mount Marcy is now one of the more popular winter outings in the Adirondacks. As big and committing as this mountain is, it has the friendly feel of a "people's mountain." I have met old ladies out for a pleasant ski tour here, alongside young bucks on a mission to prove themselves. People climb the mountain with everything from snowshoes to snowboards, old wooden skis, and telemark skis. That is the spirit of Adirondack skiing: going for a stroll in the mountains, whatever your conveyance, is an honored pastime. What is important is that you go, not how you go.

The Mount Marcy tour starts at Adirondack Loj and goes through Marcy Dam. As with the tour to Avalanche Pass, you have a choice of two routes to Marcy Dam: The most direct route (2.1 miles to Marcy Dam) is to take the Van Hoevenberg Trail from the ADK High Peaks Information Center, near Adirondack Loj. This trail, named for Adirondack Loj founder Henry Van Hoevenberg, is heavily used by hikers, snowshoers, and climbers, and is often icy. Many skiers prefer to follow the Marcy Dam Truck Trail from South Meadows. It is slightly longer (2.8 miles), but this graded truck trail can be skied with just a couple of inches of snow and the broad path is a fast ski. To reach the trailhead in South Meadows take the Adirondack Loj Road and turn left at 3.7 miles at the sign for South Meadows. Drive 1 mile to a parking area. The truck trail leaves from here. There is presently no fee for parking at South Meadows.

From Marcy Dam, pass the trail register and follow the blue-blazed Van Hoevenberg Trail up Mount Marcy. The trail climbs gradually until reaching a bridge across Phelps Brook at 3.5 miles (mileage is from the High Peaks Information Center). This is traditionally where you stop to put on climbing skins. The trail climbs steeply for the next mile until you arrive at Indian Falls. From the waterfall, there are dramatic views of Algonquin Peak with its prominent slides, as well as the neighboring summits of Boundary, Iroquois, and Wright Peak.

The Van Hoevenberg Trail moderates from here, climbing more gradually through a fir and spruce forest. Signs warn that the trail is for skis or snowshoes only, which helps keep it in good shape. A 6.4 miles, you arrive at a former lean-to site (since removed) known as the Plateau. From here, the Marcy summit cone looks immense. Like a giant vanilla ice-cream scoop scraping against the sky, Marcy appears to offer unlimited descent routes.

Continue climbing steeply through scrubby vegetation, passing the junction with the Phelps Trail at 6.8 miles. You are now at the base of the summit cone. The final half-mile is above treeline and exposed to the full force of the weather. In foggy or snowy conditions, the summit area is extremely disorienting. You should assess the weather conditions and the energy level of the members of your group before proceeding. Be especially careful to protect any exposed skin from wind, and have goggles for eye and face protection. Suit up in storm gear before leaving the last trees. You will probably not be able to see any trail markings or cairns, so good visibility is crucial up here. Climb to the summit wherever you find good snow that is out of the wind.

From the summit of Mount Marcy, the views seem limitless. Haystack and Skylight appear as huge white domes that beckon climbers and skiers. The Green Mountains are silhouetted in the distance to the east, and you peer out upon miles of roadless forest and summits. It seems incongruous that you are standing on the roof of New York, one of the most populous states in the nation.

There was once a stone hut on the summit of Mount Marcy which was popular with skiers. The structure was built in 1928 and was designed and paid for by the chairman of the Adirondack Mountain Club. Jim Goodwin, a longtime Adirondack guide who began skiing in the Adirondacks in the 1920s, told me that the hut "got a lot of action, especially for spring skiing." He explained, "People would stay in the hut and ski down to timberline and back. It really was attractive skiing, and colorful as well." But conservationists viewed the hut as a violation of the sacred "forever wild" laws that govern the Adirondacks. The matter was settled sometime

Skiing the summit cone of Mount Marcy, New York's highest peak.

during the 1940s, when the hut was struck by lightning and partially destroyed. In the 1950s, rangers finished what nature started, completely dismantling the structure. There is no trace of the famous stone hut today.

The descent of Mount Marcy is where the mountain offers up a rich multi-course offering of treats. The summit cone is brimming with secret shots and hidden ravines where you can troll for powder on your way down. You can retrace your climbing tracks (recommended in low visibility), and swing down through a beautiful steep bowl. The north face (skier's left of the hiking trail) offers a number of long ski lines, but you must take care to traverse right at the bottom in order to rejoin the trail.

Once back on the Van Hoevenberg Trail at treeline, hang on for a high-speed, heel-snapping descent through Romper Room. This narrow, winding section through scrub trees delivers you back to the saddle between Mount Marcy and Little Marcy. Several long stretches of fast trail skiing soon bring you to the Plateau. From here, climb and descend on rolling terrain, then hang on as the trail drops again. This is the Corkscrew, a 10-foot-wide section of trail that spirals back and forth down the fall line. It ends with a hard right turn and a good run-out where you can dump speed.

The Van Hoevenberg Trail continues descending steadily until Indian Falls. Below the falls is the crux of the descent: a mile-long, 6- to 8-foot-wide pipeline that charges relentlessly downhill. This pitch ends at a hard right turn onto the bridge over Phelps Brook. If you are really on it, you can ski across the bridge at full throttle. Otherwise, prepare to hit the brakes and cross the brook under control. The remaining 1.4 miles to Marcy Dam are fast, fun cruising where you can stand on your skis or snowboard and enjoy the ride (but stay alert for open drainages). Of course, standing on your skis may be all you are able to do at this point, having long since wrung the last turns from your tired legs. From Marcy Dam, it is a rolling ski back to your car.

There is a rollicking drop-and-roll rhythm to skiing the Van Hoevenberg Trail, with frequent run outs that appear magically—and just when you need them. The trail is moderately steep and averages between 6 and 10 feet wide. It calls for quick telemark or parallel turns. In good conditions, less experienced skiers can manage much of the trail with a solid snowplow. The final 2 miles on flatter ground add a nice cross-country finish to the tour.

Conditions on the Van Hoevenberg Trail actually improve with increased traffic. The more skiers, snowshoers, and snowboards pass through, the better groomed the trail gets and the easier it is to ski. Of course, a powder run is nice too, but breaking trail uphill for 7 miles is no picnic. Some of the finest skiing and riding on Mount Marcy is in April, when warm weather and spring corn snow make both the climb and descent eminently enjoyable.

The thrill of a Mount Marcy ski tour lies in its variety: skiers and riders will empty their bag of tricks negotiating the mountain. Mount Marcy calls upon the full range of ski skills, from skating the flats, to climbing uphill, to negotiating an exposed summit, to linking quick turns and skiing powder, crud, or whatever surprises the mountain has in store.

This is a committing, full-day trip that requires an early start and good preparation. Be prepared for full winter conditions on the summit, and be willing to abort your climb if conditions—either the weather or the energy of your group—are deteriorating. The exposed Mount Marcy summit can be an unforgiving place for the unprepared, but it is an unforgettable highlight for the skier or snowboarder who finally lays claim to this prize.

As you contemplate a climb of Mount Marcy today, savor the wisdom of one of its earliest pioneers. As Jackrabbit Johannsen mused:

> All my life I have been anxious to see what lies on the other side of the hill, and at the same time I have never failed to enjoy the scenery along the way. With all my senses 'tuned in'—sight and hearing, taste and smell and touch—I was able to reap full benefit from each experience. So, I say, set your goals high, and stick to them, but approach them step by step so that at any given time your expectations are not impossibly out of reach. Climb your mountain slowly, one step at a time, following a well-planned route. And when at last you stand upon the summit, you can look beyond, to the farthest horizon!

22

Thunderbolt Ski Trail, Mount Greylock, Mass.

THE TOUR

The Thunderbolt Ski Trail was one of the most famous ski race courses of the thirties and forties. It drops more than 1,800 vertical feet in 1.6 miles, beginning just below the summit of Mount Greylock. It ends at Thiel Farm in Adams.

LENGTH

1.6 miles (Thunderbolt Trail); 2.0 miles (Mount Greylock summit to Thiel Farm via Thunderbolt)

ELEVATION

Start/finish: 1,300 feet (Thiel Farm)

Highest point: 3,491 feet (Mount Greylock summit); 3,110 feet (top of Thunderbolt)

Vertical drop: 2,191 feet (from summit)

MAPS

* *Mount Greylock State Reservation* (Appalachian Mountain Club)
* *Mount Greylock Reservation Trail Map* (New England Cartographics)
* USGS North Adams (1988)

DIFFICULTY

Most difficult

SNOWBOARDING

The Thunderbolt is an excellent backcountry snowboarding descent. You will need snowshoes for the climb, and courage and finesse for the descent.

HOW TO GET THERE

To Thunderbolt trailhead: From the McKinley Monument on MA 8 in the center of Adams, drive west up Maple Street to the end. Turn left onto West Road for

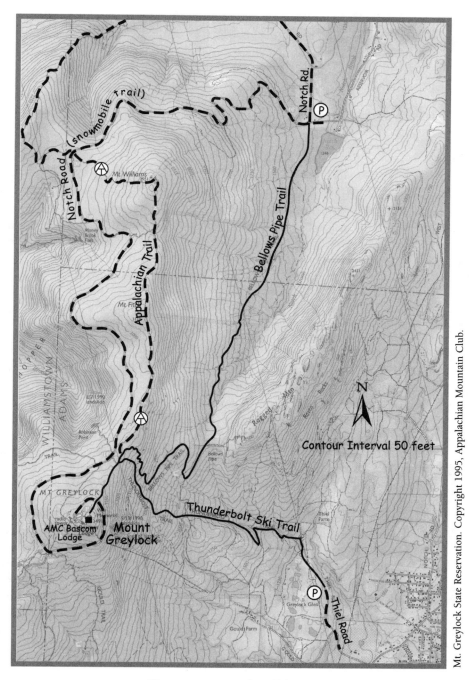

Contour Interval 50 feet

THUNDERBOLT SKI TRAIL

Mt. Greylock State Reservation. Copyright 1995, Appalachian Mountain Club.

0.4 mile, pass a crossroad sign, and turn right on Gould Road (paved, no sign). Bear right at a fork onto Thiel Road (sign says Thiel Road–Thunderbolt Trail Head) and park where plowing ends. See trail directions below.

To Bellows Pipe trailhead: From MA 2 just west of North Adams center, take Notch Road (entrance opposite gas station and cemetery), bearing left after 2.1 miles at a T-intersection, and follow it to a 90-degree corner where plowing ends. Notch Road (unplowed snowmobile route to the summit) leaves sharply right, and the Bellows Pipe Trail goes straight ahead (south).

The Thunderbolt. The intimidating name brings a smile to the face of older skiers. It is described in awestruck terms in a 1939 guidebook to eastern skiing as "one of the steepest and most difficult expert trails in the East." The ski trail up the highest mountain in Massachusetts (3,491 feet) was designed by Charlie Parker, a former caretaker of Bascom Lodge and avid skier. This lodge on the summit of Mount Greylock is now operated by the Appalachian Mountain Club and is open from April through October.

Mount Greylock was first skied in 1908 by Irving Langmuir, from Schenectady, New York. It was undoubtedly a rugged expedition, as there were no ski trails on the mountain at that time. Langmuir is better known as the winner of the Nobel Prize for chemistry in 1932. He was also one of the first and most prolific ski mountaineers in North America in the early 1900s.

The Civilian Conservation Corps (CCC) provided the muscle to turn Charlie Parker's idea for a race trail on Mount Greylock into reality. Company 107 of the CCC, based in Savoy, Massachusetts, began building the ski trail in August 1934. Three months later, national downhill ski champion Joseph Duncan visited the mountain and viewed the run. He promptly declared that the Thunderbolt was "undoubtedly the most thrilling wooded ski run in the country," according to the excellent documentary film *Purple Mountain Majesty: A History of the Thunderbolt Ski Trail*. The trail was named after an exciting roller-coaster ride in Revere Beach, outside Boston.

The Thunderbolt quickly attracted a loyal following among New England skiers. It was one of a small number of Class A ski-racing trails in the Northeast, and as such it became the scene of numerous national and regional championship races (among the other Class A trails were the Nose Dive at Stowe, Wildcat Trail in Pinkham Notch, and the Richard Taft Trail on Cannon Mountain). Class A trails had to be 1–1.5 miles long, with a vertical drop of 2,000 feet and at least one section with a gradient of 30 to 35 degrees. Top racers could earn a coveted rating with a good run here: skiing the Thunderbolt in less than three minutes made one an "A" racer; between three and four minutes qualified one as a "B" racer; and a "C" rating went to those who could schuss it in four to six minutes. The first race was held on the trail on February 16, 1935. It was won by legendary Dartmouth skier Dick Durrance in two minutes, forty-nine seconds. The course record on the Thunderbolt is two minutes, eight seconds, set by Per Klippgen at the 1948 Eastern Championships.

The Thunderbolt was much more than a ski trail. Built soon after the Great Depression, it formed the hub of a skiing subculture. Ski races became festive community events for the depressed mill town of Adams. A number of local ski clubs made the pilgrimage to the summit of Greylock every weekend, including the Mount Greylock Ski Club, the Thunderbolt Ski Club, and the Ski Runners of Adams, as well as local college teams from Williams and Amherst colleges. According to people who were regulars on the trail in the 1930s, a typical weekend crowd on the Thunderbolt would average about forty skiers, with more on weekends preceding a big race. Skiers would sidestep up the trail, packing the snow on the big turns so it wouldn't get scraped off, and "filling the bathtubs" of skiers who fell. The first race on the Thunderbolt drew a crowd of 3,500 spectators, while subsequent races drew up to 6,000 people. Spectators would line the trail and often take part in the trail-packing. Throngs of visitors would arrive on the ski trains that came from New York and Boston.

The Thunderbolt spawned a ski craze in Adams. As more townspeople were drawn to take part in the social and athletic goings-on on the east side of Mount Greylock, a local furniture store began selling skis. As *Purple Mountain Majesty* recounts, a pair of Groswold wood skis cost $22.50, more than double the weekly paycheck of local millworkers. The furniture store owner would let people pay in $1 installments. Some historic highlights on the Thunderbolt included the 1938 Eastern Amateur Downhill race, which featured an appearance by a top German ski team sent over by Adolf Hitler. The Germans won handily, defeating local ski hero Rudy Konieczny. Konieczny would meet the Germans again as a mountain soldier in the Tenth Mountain Division fighting in Italy, where he was killed in combat. Rudy's Thunderbolt buddies still speak in awe of the graceful and talented young man who inspired and challenged a generation of Adams skiers. In June 1999, the friends and family of Rudy Konieczny dedicated a stone hut on the summit of Mount Greylock in his memory.

The original Thunderbolt race course started from the summit of Mount Greylock and traveled a short distance down what is now the Appalachian Trail. It then banked east onto the current start of the trail. Running parallel to the Thunderbolt was the Bellows Pipe Trail (sometimes referred to as the Bellows Pipeline), which was considered an intermediate ski run. The upper section of the Bellows Pipe still exists, but the easy trail that today runs southeast from Notch Road to where it turns sharply uphill past a lean-to (now called the Bellows Pipe) was not part of the original trail. The lower section of the Bellows Pipe ran parallel to the Thunderbolt for its entire length and is now abandoned. On days when the Thunderbolt was too icy to safely race on, officials would detour racers onto the upper portion of the Bellows Pipe.

Skiers and snowboarders of today can test their talents on the Thunderbolt and get a humbling taste of what inspired an earlier generation of skiers more than a half-century ago. Don't expect a geriatric meander, though: this trail is for skiers who like a lot of vertical drop in a short distance. It is an exhilarating steep run that will keep you swooping through turns throughout its entire length.

Most people ski the Thunderbolt by climbing it from the bottom. To reach the bottom of the trail from where you park, ski on the unplowed Thiel Road for 0.75 mile to a small parking area with a sign that says Thunderbolt Ski Trail. This is the former Thiel Farm, which was purchased by local ski clubs in the 1930s and given to the state to serve as a skier's parking lot. Pass the sign and take the trail (marked by blue blazes) as it follows a small brook on the right. Eventually you come to a fork in the trail. A sign here directs you to the left for the Bellows Pipe Trail, and another sign says Thunderbolt Foot Trail, leading to the right. Continue following the signs for Thunderbolt Foot Trail until you reach the bottom of the ski trail. The ski trail climbs steeply, passing a cutoff at 0.8 mile where an old access road heads 0.3 mile north to connect with the Bellows Pipe Trail. At 1.6 miles, the Thunderbolt ends at a junction with the Appalachian Trail (AT). For those interested in retracing the original route of the Thunderbolt races, the summit of the mountain (along with a large war memorial tower, the AMC Bascom Lodge, and a paved road) can be reached by following the AT 0.4 mile southwest.

Bill Linscott, 1942 state champion on the Thunderbolt, recalls that the run from the summit begins with a bang. He recounts how racers would start at the summit, quickly cross Rockwell Road, and then hang on for the sharp right turn onto the Thunderbolt, which drops off precipitously. "You would come off that road and be in the air for 50 feet—and that was if you weren't trying to get air. If you jumped, you'd go a lot further," he recalls.

Dropping into the Thunderbolt from the summit is dramatic. A nondescript spur leaves the AT, and just 50 yards beyond, the whole side of the mountain falls away, revealing unobstructed views of the Berkshires and the southern peaks of the Green Mountains. Lying before you is the impressive beginning of the Thunderbolt.

The legions of skiers who lived to ski the Thunderbolt had names for every turn and dip on it—that was part of its cachet. The start of the trail at the AT was called the Big Turn, because it was the first committing turn after bombing down from the summit. The trail then hits the Big Bend, where it turns sharply and steeply east. After a long southerly traverse where the trail drops over two to three ledge steps (these can be icy), the trail enters what is still dubbed respectfully the Needle's Eye. This is the crux of the Thunderbolt. The trail narrows here and turns to the left, although the slope banks downhill into the woods. "If a skier came down and hit the Needle's Eye full tilt and didn't make the turn, he was in deep

Crowds watch a racer cross the finish line on the Thunderbolt Ski Trail, 1938.
Photo courtesy of Bill Linscott.

trouble," muses Linscott. Just beyond the Needle's Eye is the Big Schuss, the steepest drop on the trail. At one time a rope tow was operated on the Big Schuss; the snatch block for it can still be seen high up in a tree at the top of the slope.

At the bottom of the Big Schuss (0.75 mile down from the AT), a somewhat obscure connector trail leaves to the left. This leads back to the Bellows Pipe and should be taken by those making a loop trip back to Notch Road. This connecting trail was once known as the Apple Tree Trail because of a large apple tree that stood in the center of the path. Descending the Bellows Pipe back to Notch Road, be alert for numerous drainage divots on the trail, some of which may be open.

The lower section of the Thunderbolt continues to the right at the bottom of the Big Schuss (there is a sign on a large birch tree). From here to the finish line, ski racers of the past still had to contend with the Bumps, so named for the eight to ten large bumps that had to be negotiated. Then they would head into the S Turn, and ski the Last Drop, the final steep pitch before crossing the brook to the finish line.

To Linscott, who was sixteen years old when he won the championship, the memory of skiing the Thunderbolt is still fresh. "By the time you hit the S Turn, your legs are gone and your wobbly knees are bumping up and down....You were awfully glad to see the finish line when it came. Most skiers could just about stand up at the end."

World War II marked the end of the Thunderbolt's heyday. Many of the young people who had flocked to the mountain went off to fight in the war. They returned to tackle new adventures, namely raising families and finding jobs. The lure of lift-serviced downhill ski areas further dampened interest in the venerable old trail. A proposal to create a commercial ski area on the east side of Mount Grey-lock in the 1970s died. The Thunderbolt started to grow in, and by the early 1980s ski traffic on Greylock was reduced to a trickle. It looked as though the Thunderbolt was destined for the scrap bin of ski history.

But in the 1990s, the Thunderbolt got a reprieve. Suddenly a new generation of local devotees has appeared to maintain the trail, clearing underbrush and restoring it to its original width. The trail is now 20 to 40 feet wide, with open woods on either side. In good conditions, it is a playground for telemarkers, alpine skiers, and snowboarders.

The main limiting factor for skiing the Thunderbolt these days is the fickle snow conditions in western Massachusetts. The best advice for getting a good run on the Thunderbolt is to go when it snows. You will be well rewarded for seizing the moment: a powder day on the Thunderbolt is still as good as skiing gets. And skiing or snowboarding this legendary run will give you new respect for your elders.

As you descend this epic run today, allow your mind to drift. Picture yourself shadowing a 1930s racer down the Thunderbolt. The skier clad in wool knickers is bearing down the mountain on his long wooden boards. His baggy clothes flap hysterically in the wind. Friends cheer as his skis chatter through the Needle's Eye, down the Big Schuss, over the Bumps, and through the S Turn. You follow, hang-ing on as you hurdle through history.

The sidelines of the Thunderbolt are quiet again. Only the sound of your skis or snowboard slicing through fresh powder breaks the silence of the woods now. The legends of this run are tucked neatly beneath the snowy mantle. But as you descend this great mountain, you can still feel the same trepidation and reverence that earlier skiers felt for this old trail.

This Thunderbolt, as you will discover, is still electrifying.

OTHER OPTIONS

You can also reach the Thunderbolt by including it as part of a longer, more mod-erate ski tour on the Bellows Pipe Trail. From Notch Road, the lower section of the modern-day Bellows Pipe offers easy cross-country skiing through gentle terrain.

The Bellows Pipe climbs gradually until you reach a junction at 2.6 miles, marked by orange flashing. The trail turns sharply right (northwest) here, passes a lean-to, and climbs steeply up seven switchbacks. Several abandoned trails leave south to connect with the Thunderbolt, but the Bellows Pipe continues up until it meets the AT. The sign marking the start of the Thunderbolt is on the AT, 0.1 mile south of the Bellows Pipe–AT junction. On your descent, retrace your tracks on the Bellows Pipe. Alternatively, you can ski Notch Road up Mount Greylock, which is used by snowmobiles. It is a long, gentle downhill for those wishing to ski to the summit and back, but it is often icy due to the heavy snowmobile use.

Another excellent and challenging down-mountain route for backcountry skiing or snowboarding is the historic Stony Ledge Trail on the west side of Mount Greylock. It can be reached from the trails of the Mount Greylock Ski Club (trail conditions: 413-445-7887, www.berkshireweb.com/plexus/sports/mtgreylock. html), located off MA 7 on Roaring Brook Road, just south of Williamstown.

POSTSCRIPT

Protecting Our Wildlands

This book is about the past, the present, and—most importantly—the future of skiing. Skiers and snowboarders are picking up where earlier generations left off and are returning to the backcountry. The possibilities of where we can go and what we can explore are almost limitless.

Our opportunity to travel freely in the backcountry cannot be taken for granted. The northeastern wilderness is shrinking, as large swaths of land are traded and sold to speculators and large timber companies. The Northern Forest, covering 26 million acres of land stretching from Maine to the Adirondacks, is under threat. It is an area that is home to a million people and within a day's drive of 70 million more.

Eighty-five percent of the Northern Forest is privately owned. Between 1998 and 2000, more than 6 million acres of the Northern Forest were sold, some of it to foreign investors. In Maine alone, 18 percent of the state's land was sold during that time. Clearcutting is still a problem—60,000 acres of Maine forest were leveled just in 1992. There is also a great risk of large undeveloped areas being chopped up and sold off as small real-estate parcels. The habitat of backcountry skiers—the high and wild places all around us—is at risk.

Backcountry users should be part of the solution. The Northern Forest Alliance is working to create a sustainable future for the vast Northern Forest. The alliance has proposed the creation of ten wildlands across the Northeast. These areas range from a 1.3-million-acre protected swath around Baxter State Park in Maine to a 160,000-acre preserve in the western Adirondacks. This is a visionary yet practical effort that may be our last opportunity to protect millions of acres of precious wilderness. The wildlands are intended to "maintain ecological balance, provide remote and wilderness recreation opportunities, provide solitude to rekindle the spirit, and support the region's forest-based economy."

You can help. Support the wildlands efforts near you. To find out who is working to protect the areas where you like to ski, contact the Northern Forest Alliance, 43 State Street, Montpelier, VT 05602; 802-223-5256; www.thenorthernforest.org.

Value the backcountry enough to preserve it. Work with local environmental groups and land trusts to protect access to our wildlands. You might just discover your next favorite ski tour in land you helped save.

APPENDIX A

Outdoor and Instructional Organizations

Following is a selective listing of organizations in the Northeast that offer information or instructional programs related to backcountry skiing, winter mountaineering, and wilderness first aid. This is by no means a comprehensive list. Most downhill ski areas and ski-touring centers now offer telemark lessons in addition to other classes. Snowboard lessons are available at any downhill ski area.

Adirondack Mountain Club
814 Goggins Road
Lake George, NY 12845
518-668-4447
www.adk.org

The ADK offers a variety of courses on winter skills, as well as guided trips. The ADK also publishes the most authoritative guidebooks about the Adirondacks. The annual AMC-ADK winter mountaineering school provides an excellent introduction to the skills you need to travel safely in the winter wilderness.

Adirondack Ski Touring Council
P.O. Box 843
Lake Placid, NY 12946
518-523-1365 (24-hour information and trail conditions)

The Adirondack Ski Touring Council oversees the Jackrabbit Trail, the 35-mile ski trail that links the towns of Paul Smiths, Saranac Lake, Lake Placid, and Keene. The Jackrabbit Trail includes both groomed and backcountry sections. It travels through five cross-country ski centers and wilderness areas in the Adirondacks. The ASTC offers a free topographic map of the entire Jackrabbit Trail.

Appalachian Mountain Club
5 Joy Street
Boston, MA 02108
617-523-0636 (Boston) or 603-466-2727 (Pinkham Notch, NH)
www.outdoors.org

The AMC offers courses throughout the winter in telemark and backcountry skiing, avalanche assessment, ski touring, and mountain safety. The AMC also offers an extensive selection of guidebooks and maps for all of the Northeast.

Catamount Trail Association
1 Main Street
Burlington, VT 05401
802-864-5794
www.catamounttrail.together.com

The Catamount Trail is a 300-mile backcountry ski trail that runs the length of Vermont. It links eleven cross-country centers along the way. The Catamount Trail Association offers maps, information, and an excellent guidebook (see appendix B) about the trail.

Green Mountain Club
4711 Waterbury-Stowe Road
Waterbury Center, VT 05677
802-244-7037
www.greenmountainclub.org

The Green Mountain Club is the steward of Vermont's 270-mile Long Trail. It sponsors a variety of outdoor educational lectures and workshops. It is also a resource for maps and guidebooks about the Vermont backcountry.

Hurricane Island Outward Bound School
75 Mechanic Street
Rockland, ME 04841
800-341-1744
www.hurricaneisland.org

The Hurricane Island Outward Bound School offers a wide range of winter courses in the White Mountains of New Hampshire and in the Mahoosuc Mountains of Maine. These courses provide a comprehensive introduction to winter skills, including winter mountaineering, backcountry skiing, and wilderness navigation.

North American Telemark Organization (NATO)
Box 44
Waitsfield, VT 05673
800-835-3404
www.telemarknato.com

Dick Hall is the grandmaster of telemark and backcountry ski instruction. Nobody teaches people the basics of cross-country downhill technique as well, and with as much enthusiasm, as he and his NATO instructors do. NATO offers courses all around the Northeast for skiers ranging from beginner to expert and people interested in multiday adventure tours.

Stonehearth Open Learning Opportunities (SOLO)
P.O. Box 3150
Conway, NH 03818
603-447-6711
www.stonehearth.com

SOLO offers backcountry first-aid programs, including Wilderness Emergency Medical Technician and Wilderness First Responder courses.

Wilderness Medical Associates
189 Dudley Road
Bryant Pond, ME 04219
888-945-3633
www.wildmed.com

Wilderness Medical Associates offers a full complement of backcountry medicine courses, from weekend first-aid classes to Wilderness Emergency Medical Technician courses.

APPENDIX B

Recommended Reading

AVALANCHE SAFETY

Daffern, Tony. *Avalanche Safety for Skiers and Climbers*. 2d ed. Seattle: The Mountaineers, 1992.

Fredston, Jill and Doug Fesler. *Snow Sense: A Guide to Evaluating Snow Avalanche Hazard*. Anchorage, Ala.: Alaska Mountain Safety Center, 1994.

LaChapelle, E. R. *The ABC of Avalanche Safety*. 2d ed. Seattle: The Mountaineers, 1985.

FIRST AID

Hubbell, Frank, and Buck Tilton. *Medicine for the Backcountry*. 2d ed. Merrillville, Ind.: ICS Books, 1994.

Lentz, Martha, Steven Macdonald, and Jan Carline. *Mountaineering First Aid*. 4th ed. Seattle: The Mountaineers, 1996.

GUIDEBOOKS—NORTHEAST TRAILS

Adirondack Mountain Club. *Guide to Adirondack Trails: High Peaks Region*. 12th ed. Lake George, N.Y.: Adirondack Mountain Club, 1992.

Appalachian Mountain Club. *Maine Mountain Guide*. 8th ed. Boston: Appalachian Mountain Club Books, 1999.

Appalachian Mountain Club. *White Mountain Guide*. 26th ed. Boston: Appalachian Mountain Club Books, 1998.

Appalachian Mountain Club. *Southern New Hampshire Trail Guide*, 1st ed. Boston: Appalachian Mountain Club Books, 1999.

Appalachian Mountain Club. *Massachusetts and Rhode Island Trail Guide*, 7th ed. Boston: Appalachian Mountain Club Books, 1999.

Green Mountain Club. *Long Trail Guide*. 24th ed. Waterbury Center, Vt.: Green Mountain Club, 1996.

GUIDEBOOKS—BACKCOUNTRY SKIING AND SNOWBOARDING IN NORTH AMERICA

Burgdorfer, Rainer. *100 Classic Backcountry Ski & Snowboard Routes in Washington*. Seattle: The Mountaineers, 1999.

Catamount Trail Association. *The Catamount Trail Guidebook*. 7th ed. Burlington, Vt.: Catamount Trail Association, 1999.

Dawson, Louis W. *Colorado 10th Mountain Huts and Trails*. Aspen, Colo.: WHO Press, 1998.

Dawson, Louis W. *Dawson's Guide to Colorado Backcountry Skiing*: Volume 1, Independence Pass, Aspen, Glenwood Springs. Colorado Springs, Colo.: Blue Clover Press, 2000.

Dawson, Louis W. *Wild Snow: 54 Classic Ski and Snowboard Descents of North America*. Golden, Colo.: American Alpine Club Press, 1998.

Goodwin, Tony. *Classic Adirondack Ski Tours*. Lake George, N.Y.: Adirondack Mountain Club, 1994.

Moynier, John. *Backcountry Skiing California's High Sierra*. Helena, Mont.: Falcon Books, 1999.

Richins, Paul Jr. *50 Classic Backcountry Ski & Snowboard Summits in California*. Seattle: The Mountaineers, 1999.

Scofield, Bruce, Christopher Ryan, and Nancy Prajzner. *Skiing the Pioneer Valley: Cross-Country Ski Centers, Backcountry Touring, and Downhill Ski Areas*. Amherst, Mass.: New England Cartographics, 1997.

Scott, Chic. *Ski Trails in the Canadian Rockies*. Calgary: Rocky Mountain Books, 1992.

Scott, Chic. *Summits & Icefields: Alpine Ski Tours in the Rockies and Columbia Mountains of Canada*. Calgary: Rocky Mountain Books, 1994.

MOUNTAINEERING SKILLS

Gorman, Stephen. *AMC Guide to Winter Camping*. 2d ed. Boston: Appalachian Mountain Club Books, 1999.

Graydon, Don, and Kurt Hanson, eds. *Mountaineering: The Freedom of the Hills*. 6th ed. Seattle: The Mountaineers, 1997.

Lanza, Michael. *Ultimate Guide to Backcountry Travel*. Boston: Appalachian Mountain Club Books, 1999.

SKI AND SNOWBOARD TECHNIQUE

Parker, Paul. *Free-Heel Skiing: Telemark and Parallel Techniques for All Conditions.* Seattle: The Mountaineers, 1995.

Van Tilburg, Christopher. *Backcountry Snowboarding.* Seattle: The Mountaineers, 1998.

SKI HISTORY

Allen, E. John B. *From Skisport to Skiing: One Hundred Years of an American Sport, 1840–1940.* Amherst: University of Massachusetts Press, 1995.

Allen, E. John B. *New England Skiing.* Dover, N.H.: Arcadia Publishing, 1997.

Federal Writers' Project. *Skiing in the East: The Best Trails and How to Get There.* 1939 ed. Irvine, Calif.: Reprint Services Corp., [n.d.].

Johannsen, Alice E. *The Legendary Jackrabbit Johannsen.* Montreal: McGill-Queen's University Press, 1993.

Pote, Winston. *Mount Washington in Winter: Photographs and Recollections 1923–1940.* Camden, Maine: Down East Books, 1985 (out of print).

Waterman, Laura and Guy. *Forest and Crag: A History of Hiking, Trail Blazing, and Adventure in the Northeast Mountains.* Boston: Appalachian Mountain Club Books, 1989.

MAPS

The best hiking and skiing maps of Vermont are published by Map Adventures. The two maps that cover many of the Vermont tours in this book are *Northern Vermont Adventure Skiing* and *Vermont–New Hampshire Hiking.* Contact Map Adventures: 802-253-7480, www.mapadventures.com.

The authoritative maps of the Adirondacks are published by the Adirondack Mountain Club (ADK). *Trails of the Adirondack High Peaks Region* covers all the New York ski tours in this book. The ADK also publishes a full set of maps covering other parts of the Adirondacks. Order from the ADK: 800-395-8080, www.adk.org.

Adirondack Maps publishes the large map *The Adirondacks: High Peaks Region.* This map covers from Paul Smiths to Elizabethtown, and is available in many convenience stores in northern New York. Adirondack Maps also publishes maps covering other parts of the Adirondacks. Contact Adirondack Maps: 518-576-9861, www.adirondackmaps.com.

For navigating the back roads of the Northeast, the DeLorme *Atlas & Gazetteer* is indispensable. The editions for Vermont and New York are available from DeLorme: 800-452-5931, www.delorme.com.

The Vermont Road Atlas and Guide by Northern Cartographic will get you to your Vermont trailhead, no matter how far out on a back road it is. Contact Northern Cartographic: 802-860-2886, www.northerncartographic.com.

AMC topographic maps are the best general maps for skiing in New Hampshire, Maine, and Massachusetts. Contact the AMC: 800-262-4455, www.outdoors.org.

USGS topographic maps are now available on CD-ROM. Vermont, Adirondack Park, and Massachusetts are covered by one CD-ROM for each area. Contact Maptech: 800-627-7236, www.maptech.com.

USGS maps (on paper) are also available directly from the U.S. Geological Survey. USGS also publishes useful informational pamphlets on using its maps. Contact USGS: 800-USA-MAPS, www.usgs.gov.

APPENDIX C

Lodging and Travel Information

Following are contacts for information on tourism, lodging, and attractions in Vermont and the Adirondack region of New York.

Adirondack Mountain Club
518-523-3441
www.adk.org

The Adirondack Mountain Club (ADK) operates Adirondack Loj, a rustic mountain inn in the heart of the Adirondack Mountains, five miles south of Lake Placid. The Loj, built in 1927, has space for forty-six guests, and frequently hosts outdoor educational activities. The ADK also operates the backcountry hut Camp Peggy O'Brien (see the Camp Peggy O'Brien Hut Tour chapter).

Adirondack Regional Tourism Council
800-487-6867
www.adk.com

Provides a wealth of information on lodging, events, and tourism throughout the Adirondack region of New York.

Lake Placid/Essex County Convention and Visitors Bureau
800-44PLACID
www.lakeplacid.com

For lodging, travel, and recreation information on the High Peaks region of the Adirondacks, including Lake Placid and Keene.

New York State Division of Tourism
www.iloveny.com
800-CALLNYS

The official travel information gateway for the state of New York. Provides listings for most accommodations in the state, as well as general travel information.

Stowe Area Association
877-GOSTOWE
www.gostowe.com

Stowe Area Association offers lodging, dining, and travel information for the area in and around Stowe, Vermont.

Vermont Department of Tourism and Marketing
800-VERMONT
www.1-800-vermont.com

The official travel and tourism gateway for the state of Vermont, with links and information about lodging and recreation. Distributes the free annual publication, *Vermont Winter Guide,* with listings and articles about statewide attractions.

APPENDIX D

Emergency Contacts

VERMONT

Vermont State Police
911 (in-state) or 802-244-8727 (out of state)

NEW YORK (ADIRONDACK STATE PARK)

Department of Environmental Conservation—Emergency Dispatch
518-891-0235

About the Author

David Goodman is a writer, skier, and mountaineer who has written widely about the outdoors and other subjects. He is a contributing editor for *Ski* and *Back Country* magazines. His articles have appeared in *Outside, National Geographic Adventure, Sports Afield, Men's Journal*, and other national publications. He is a three-time winner of the Harold S. Hirsch Award for Excellence in Ski Writing, the highest award of the North American Ski Journalists Association—twice for his magazine writings and once for *Classic Backcountry Skiing: A Guide to the Best Ski Tours in New England*. He is also a recipient of the International Ski History Association's Ullr Award for his writings on ski history in *Classic Backcountry Skiing*.

Goodman is also the author of the critically acclaimed book *Fault Lines: Journeys into the New South Africa* (University of California Press, 1999). His investigative and feature articles have appeared in *The Washington Post, Mother Jones, The Village Voice, The Nation*, and other publications.

David Goodman is a graduate of Harvard University. He has worked as a mountaineering instructor for Outward Bound and is a Wilderness Emergency Medical Technician.

While his travels have taken him to five continents, Goodman still insists that his favorite place to explore is in his backyard—the mountains of the Northeast. He lives with his wife and two children in northern Vermont.

About the Appalachian Mountain Club

BEGIN A NEW ADVENTURE!

Join the Appalachian Mountain Club, the oldest and largest outdoor recreation club in the United States. Since 1876, the Appalachian Mountain Club has helped people experience the majesty and solitude of the Northeast outdoors. Our mission is to promote the protection, enjoyment, and wise use of the mountains, rivers, and trails of the Appalachian region. We're committed to responsible outdoor recreation and we spearhead conservation and environmental efforts in the Northeast and mid-Atlantic areas.

Members enjoy discounts on all AMC programs, facilities, and books.

Outdoor Adventure Programs

We offer more than 100 workshops on hiking, canoeing, cross-country skiing, biking, and rock climbing, and guided trips for hikers, canoers, and skiers.

Mountain Huts and Visitor Centers

The AMC maintains backcountry huts in the White Mountains of New Hampshire and visitor centers throughout the Northeast, from Maine to New Jersey.

Books and Maps

We publish guidebooks and maps to the mountains, streams, and forests of the Appalachian region—from Maine to North Carolina—and outdoor-skills books written by backcountry experts on topics from winter camping to fly-fishing. Call 800-262-4455 to order AMC books or to receive a complete catalog.

To learn more about our workshops, facilities, books, conservation efforts, and membership benefits, contact us at:

Appalachian Mountain Club
5 Joy Street
Boston, MA 02108
617-523-0636

Visit our website: www.outdoors.org.

You'll never find this in bounds.

Black Diamond has been skiing the backcountry and making the best backcountry ski gear since 1984. For over a decade, we have developed the most reliable and innovative products to make your backcountry ski experience the best it can be. For the most comprehensive line of backcountry ski equipment in the world, see your local Black Diamond dealer or contact us directly at ski@bdel.com.

◆ Black Diamond™

2084 E. 3900 S.   Salt Lake City, UT 84124   U.S.A.
801.278.5533   www.BlackDiamondEquipment.com

Skiing near Cedar Breaks, Utah. JOHN DITTLI

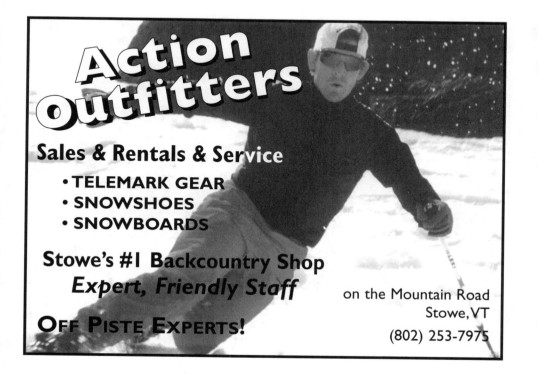